# got spirit?

# got spirit?

Practical Spiritual Wisdom
for the School of Life

Copyright © 2001

All rights reserved. No part of this book may be reproduced in any form or by any electronic or mechanical means, including information storage and retrieval systems, without permission in writing from the publisher, except by a reviewer who may quote brief passages in a review.

IAM Spirit PUBLISHING
10131 Coors Rd. NW, Ste. 1 2-886, Albuquerque, New Mexico 87114

Library of Congress Card Number: 00-111246

Cover Art and Book Layout by
Wiatt's Design, Richmond, Virginia

Manufactured in the United States.

*First Edition*
SAN: 253-1607

**Publisher's Cataloging-in-Publication**
*(Provided by Quality Books, Inc.)*

Got spirit? : practical spiritual wisdom for the school of life / contributing editor, Kay Lewis Shaw. -- 1st ed.
  p. cm.
  Includes bibliographical references.
  LCCN: 00-111246
  ISBN: 0-9678780-9-8

  1. Spiritual life. 2. Metaphysics. I. Shaw, Kay Lewis.

BL624.G68 2001            291.4
                          QBI00-998

# DEDICATION

With gratitude and thanksgiving for assisting us in our Spiritual process, we dedicate this book to all our teachers along our individual Spiritual paths but especially to Patrick Pollard, Jac Blackman, and Marje Larragoite.

*You dearest darling Patrick,*

*You have been a profound expression of Unconditional Love in my life & the lives of so many others. Thank you! Thank you! Thank you!*

*Namaste!*

*Happy*

## Publisher's Note Page

When using the word *healing,* it is to be understood by the reader that the authors, editor, or publisher do not mean a physical cure of a disease. Though in some cases a physical healing will accompany a spiritual healing. Spiritual healing in the general sense as it is represented in this book means a healing of the mind, which brings a feeling of at-one-ment or peace to the person who has originally found himself in conflict about a situation, person, or event. This type of spiritual peace or peace of mind is peace in spite of outward circumstances.

# got spirit?

*Contributing Editor:*
Kay Lewis Shaw

*Contributing Writers:*
David Alexander
Rebecca Allen
Jeannie Bullard
Lynne Curtis
Barbara Fox
David Schultz
Kay Lewis Shaw
Tammy L. Young

# TABLE OF CONTENTS

Foreword ..................................................................................... i

Introduction ............................................................................... iii
    Walking in Divinity: Healing Through
        Spiritual Principles – *David Alexander*

## Section One – Change .......................................................... 3
    Change – *Rebecca Allen*
    Thoughts About Change – *Tammy L. Young*
    **Prayer Treatment** – *Tammy L. Young*
    Change – *Barbara Fox*
    **Prayer Treatment** – *Barbara Fox*

## Section Two – Creativity ..................................................... 11
    Understanding How the Law of Creativity Works
      – *"Happy" Shaw*
    What Creative and Creativity Mean to Me – *Barbara Fox*
    Thoughts on Creativity – *Dave Schultz*
    Create, Creative and Creativity – *Jeannie Bullard*
    **Prayer Treatment** – *Barbara Fox*

## Section Three – How Prayer Treatment Works ............. 21
    How Spiritual Mind Treatment Works – *Jeannie Bullard*
    Mind-Body Connection – *Lynne Curtis*
    Using Spiritual Mind Treatment for Healing – *Rebecca Allen*
    **Prayer Treatment** – *Rebecca Allen*

## Section Four – Intuition ..................................................... 33
    How I Use Intuition – *Barbara Fox*
    **Prayer Treatment** – *"Happy" Shaw*

## Section Five – Faith ............................................................ 37
    Faith – *Rebecca Allen*
    The Origin, Nature, and Function of Faith – *"Happy" Shaw*
    Faith: That Greater Awareness – *David Alexander*

Faith or *Haymanootha* – *Jeannie Bullard*
Learning to Have Faith – *Tammy L. Young*
*Prayer Treatment* – *Tammy L. Young*

## Section Six – Prosperity......55
A Letter About Ego and Prosperity – *"Happy" Shaw*
*Prayer Treatment* – *Rebecca Allen*

## Section Seven – Integrity......61
Integrity – *Tammy L. Young*
*Prayer Treatment* – *Tammy L. Young*

## Section Eight – Death and Life......65
Abandon All Hope: A Love Story – *Lynne Curtis*
Thoughts About Living and Dying – *Barbara Fox*
Life and Death – *David Alexander*
On Death and Dying – *"Happy" Shaw*
*Prayer Treatment* – *"Happy" Shaw*

## Section Nine – Ending Addictive Behaviors......83
Ending Addictive/Compulsive Behaviors
  – *David Alexander and Rebecca Allen*
What I Believe to Be True About Addictive/Compulsive
  Behavior – *"Happy" Shaw*
*Prayer Treatment* – *Jeannie Bullard*

## Section Ten – Forgiveness......95
Forgiveness of the Past Releases the Present – *"Happy" Shaw*
*Prayer Treatment* – *"Happy" Shaw*

## Section Eleven – Oneness......101
One with God – *Rebecca Allen*
*Prayer Treatment* – *Rebecca Allen*
What It Means to Be One – *Jeannie Bullard*
Shades of Oneness – *"Happy" Shaw*
*Prayer Treatment* – *"Happy" Shaw*

## Section Twelve – Trust ........ 109

    Trust – *Tammy L. Young*
    **Prayer Treatment** – *Tammy L. Young*
    Trust – *Barbara Fox*
    Faith is Trust – *Jeannie Bullard*
    **Prayer Treatment** – *"Happy" Shaw*

## Section Thirteen – Healing ........ 119

    Thoughts About Healing – *Barbara Fox*
    Healing and Health – *Dave Schultz*
    My Healing Through the Use of Spiritual Principles – *"Happy" Shaw*
    Rediscovering Health – *Jeannie Bullard*
    **Prayer Treatment** – *Jeannie Bullard*

## Section Fourteen – The Perfection of Perceived Imperfection ........ 133

    The Perfection of Imperfection – *Lynne Curtis*
    **Prayer Treatment** – *Jeannie Bullard*

## Section Fifteen – Practicing the Presence ........ 141

    Practicing the Presence – *Rebecca Allen*
    The Art of Conscious Living – *Jeannie Bullard*
    Practicing the Presence by Ritualizing Mundane Tasks – *Jeannie Bullard, "Happy" Shaw and Barbara Fox*
    **Prayer Treatment** – *Jeannie Bullard*

## Section Sixteen – Present Moment ........ 151

    Healing Power of Living in the Present Moment – *Jeannie Bullard*
    Living in the Moment – *Dave Schultz*
    Healing Power of the Present – *Barbara Fox*

## Section Seventeen – Compassion ........ 159

    Do No Harm – *Lynne Curtis*

## Section Eighteen – Purpose ........................ 167
    Purpose – *Barbara Fox*
    *Prayer Treatment* – *Jeannie Bullard*
    Reflections on My Life's Purpose – *"Happy" Shaw*
    *Prayer Treatment* – *"Happy" Shaw*

## Section Nineteen – Wholeness ........................ 177
    The Perception of Wholeness – *Tammy L. Young*
    *Prayer Treatment* – *Tammy L. Young*

## Section Twenty –
## The Prodigal Son as Our Story ........................ 181
    The Prodigal Son as My Story – *"Happy" Shaw*
    *Prayer Treatment* – *"Happy" Shaw*

## Section Twenty-One – The Spiritual Path ........................ 191
    My Crooked Path – *Rebecca Allen*
    My Spiritual Journey: Coming to Know a
        Power Greater Than Myself – *Tammy L. Young*
    *Prayer Treatment* – *"Tammy L. Young"*

## Section Twenty-Two – Closing Prayer ........................ 205
    *Closing Prayer* – *Barbara Fox*

Authors' Bios ........................ 207
Correspondence to the Authors ........................ 209
Copyright Acknowledgments ........................ 210
Recommended Reading and Audio Tapes ........................ 211

## FOREWORD

For four years, a small group of people of all ages and of many different backgrounds committed to study metaphysical healing or "spiritual healing."

**got spirit? Practical Spiritual Wisdom for the School of Life** is the result of that years-long study. It is presented in sections, consisting of essays and prayers, centered around aspects of life in which one often is conflicted in searching for and finding the spiritual truth.

Many sections offer profoundly personal steps in the individual writer's process of spiritual growth. Often touching, humorous, academic or folksy, the essays and prayers are written in the personal speaking styles of the individual authors, letting the reader come to know the writers individually as well as collectively.

The collective name THE ALMOST SPIRITUAL MASTERS was chosen because it is the belief of the authors that one's spiritual journey is a continuing process and it often has a pattern of taking two steps forward and seemingly three backwards. Self-realization or enlightenment or awareness for most people is a continual process. However, one can reach a stage where one ceases to fall back as much as before. As in the old saying, "Before enlightenment, chop wood, tote water. After enlightenment, chop wood, tote water." the authors hope to reveal that by working in alignment with our Spiritual selves, we can make our chopping and toting holy work if we continue to rediscover ourselves as whole people through healing of any thought of separation from the God/Spirit within and around us.

Healing of our thoughts of separation or aligning ourselves with Spirit can be done through meditation or a process variously called *spiritual mind treatment or prayer treatment or affirmative prayer*. It is simply a way of praying as Jesus taught – to actively pray as if we already have that which we pray for, giving thanks for it, and letting the Law or the Holy Spirit manifest it for us. And thus, it will be done to us as we believe. There are many books which discuss the affirmative prayer process at length and the reader is referred to the list of recommended books in the back of the text.

When using the word *healing*, it is to be understood by the reader that the authors, editor, or publisher do not mean a physical cure of a disease. Though in some cases a physical healing will accompany a spiritual healing. Spiritual healing in the general sense as it is represented in this book means a healing of the mind, which brings a feeling of at-one-ment or peace to the person who has originally found himself in conflict about a situation, person, or event. This type of spiritual peace or peace of mind is peace in spite of outward circumstances.

It is the editor's and authors' hope that readers will find something of themselves in the struggles and spiritual journeys related here. First, to realize they are not alone. Second, to open their minds to the vastness of Spirit and Its power to bring a sense of wholeness, healing, and peace to their everyday lives.

December, 2001
Kay Lewis Shaw
a.k.a. "Happy" Shaw
contributing editor

## INTRODUCTION

### Walking in Divinity: Healing Through Spiritual Principles

What is Spiritual Healing? Let me illustrate with a personal story.

In November 1994, my senior year in high school, on a normal Monday night, I was driving to my girlfriend's house to pick her up. We were on our way to a tutoring session held regularly on Monday nights in our high school library.

On our way there, I felt a sharp pain in my chest which would not go away. It turned out to be caused by the collapsing of part of my right lung. I went into the hospital and had it corrected on Tuesday and was back in school on Wednesday. I was told it was a random event known as a spontaneous pneumothorax. The doctors said I had a fifteen percent chance of it ever happening again and not to worry. So, I didn't and went about my normal life.

In March of 1995 it happened again. This time I was a little more concerned about what I might have done to cause this to happen again. I spent five days in the hospital and underwent a painful procedure to correct the problem. Again I was told the chances of it happening again were very low, but it did.

Two weeks later I was back in the hospital and this time undergoing major reconstructive lung surgery!

These events gave me a chance to seriously look at my life and to try and find some answers. The doctors had no answers as to why this occurred and I was not satisfied with just being the medical wonder known as "lung boy."

So what happened? I had been reared in metaphysical religious teachings and I wondered, "What was wrong with my thinking? What negative thoughts was I repressing? What traumatic childhood experience had I not yet healed?"

To find these answers I turned inward. I meditated and contemplated for a long time and could not come up with any answers. I was getting frustrated quickly.

I had studied Dr. Ernest Holmes book *The Science of Mind's* principles at youth camps and workshops, and I had completed a great deal of inner work on my childhood experiences, thoughts and all the rest. I don't mean to say that I had cleared everything up, but it does make a difference when one has been fortunate enough to grow up in these teachings and to apply these principles to life from childhood as opposed to 20 or 40 years later.

Frankly, I was sick of hearing people talk from the Freudian paradigm, suggesting that my reoccurring illness had something to do with my mother or some other repressed event. After all growing up in metaphysical spiritual teachings, I knew everything we experience is a result of mind in action. I was beginning to think, *maybe things just happen.* Yet I had always been taught that things always happen for a reason, if for only the simple act of teaching us a lesson.

*Ahh, that's it!* I thought. A lesson, that is what this was all about, I am supposed to learn something. But what? The only thing I could come up with was "Don't take your girlfriend to study as a date, don't watch history films and try not to walk too much." These were the things that I was doing at the times it happened. Well those assumptions certainly did not quite cut it as answers. However, actually I do believe that there were some serious things to learn about my life style through these experiences.

I learned that I need to slow down, take more time for myself, appreciate life more (especially the everyday things) and put more effort into my physical health. So, I started working hard on each of these areas of my life. I set goals and expectations for myself. As I began accomplishing these things my life began to improve. I began to experience success and happiness like never before, my life really took off! I was working out at a gym, on a meal plan and balancing work with fun. I felt really good about life and that I had finally put this experience all behind me.

Summer came and went, fall approached and I returned to

## got spirit?

college. In October I went to St.Louis for the second time. I had gone out once in the summer to do a workshop at a church there for their teen group and a sermon for the church on Sunday. Now I was going back to run their teen program at the church camp.

My topic was "Walking In Divinity." I worked with the teens in developing an idea of what this might be like for each of them. One of the activities I lead them in was a guided meditation. I took them on a long journey where they had the opportunity to see how divinity might show up in their lives.

I asked them what it would look and feel like in each area of their lives and how that would be different from how it is now. I also asked them what they would have to heal in order for this change to take place. This was a very powerful experience for each of them. I was amazed at the things they saw in the meditation, but I did not realize this was going to be a transforming experience for me as well!

Just a few hours after the meditation my lung collapsed! This time it was the left lung and it was the entire lung that went down! Talk about a shocker! How could this possibly happen to me again? I thought I had learned my lesson, fixed my life and moved on.

This was the beginning of my true spiritual healing. I certainly had every right to feel upset and angry but I did not. Moments after I realized what was happening to me I was filled with a sense of peace and purpose as to what was happening. It was not until the next day in the hospital that I could really articulate what I was feeling. As people from the St. Louis church poured into my room at all hours of each day and as my phone rang with people from all over the country, I gave them all the same answer as to how I was feeling, "I am the blue sky!"

You see, during my flight to St. Louis, I was taken away by the beauty of the blue sky. Under the plane was a blanket of white clouds so smooth it looked like snow and extended forever. The sky was the most incredible blue I had ever seen. However, when the plane dropped below the clouds and into the St. Louis area, things became dark and dreary. The clouds were black and everything was wet and cold and miserable. But what occurred to me was that in spite of the appearance, this was not the Truth. The Truth was that the sky was blue and beautiful, I could just not physically see it.

When you cannot see something it does not mean that it is not there!

Dr. Ernest Holmes said that a demonstration is "made when the thing is accomplished which the one treating desires to achieve" (SOM pp174). What I wanted from the first experience was a healing, to be whole perfect and complete. The problem was that as long as I believed I was not physically perfect then I must not be spiritually. Holmes also says that we cannot demonstrate beyond our ability to mentally embody an idea.

The revelation had occurred to me that my Truth was and always is God's Perfection, despite appearances. You see, when this happened to me the first time I felt disconnected from God. I felt like I had to learn my lesson, make the appropriate changes in my life and by doing so I would be reconnected to God. It was this belief that was keeping me from having a demonstration.

This time, even in my physical pain, I felt 100 percent connected to God. I knew this was a healing because just as Dr. Holmes had said when we are healed we will not suffer but are still able to feel pain. Well, during my first three experiences, I not only felt great physical pain but also suffering. But this last time (and I do mean last) I still felt physical pain but I never suffered. The healing which had occurred was in my mind and my thinking.

I was familiar with principles which stated, "God is all there is," "Nothing exists outside the presence of God" and so forth but I knew them only in my head. I had finally taken that long eight inch journey to the heart. Once my thinking changed regarding the outward condition, I was healed. All this time I was looking for a healing of the body when all I needed was a healing of the mind – of my belief system.

And the Reality is that the only healing which was needed was the revealing of my True self, my God self, my Divinity, a revelation and new awareness that I am and always have been walking in Divinity.

**David Alexander,** Ministerial Student

*I am in every religion as a thread through a string of pearls.*

– Bhagava Gita

## got spirit?

## SECTION ONE

# *Change*

*"Behold, I set before you this day a blessing and a curse."*
— Deut. 11:26

## Change
*Rebecca Hathaway Allen*

It has been said, "people really never change." When I first gave this idea some thought, my first reaction was resistance. I know I have changed. I am not the same person I used to be – thank God. On deeper reflection, however, maybe this cliche is closer to the truth than I would have thought.

I used to be hyper, scattered and uncertain. I still have my moments, of course, but over the course of my spiritual studies, my life has taken on a rich depth that I would never have dreamed possible. Recently, I have realized I have simply found my way back to my basic nature. I have shrugged off the clutter that was masking my true self and reconnected with the person I am in the deeper sense.

Change is upsetting when we have expectations, when we project fear of future outcomes, or when we allow old business to color our present. If we stay in the moment, however, each second is only a millisecond different from the last. Staying in the present moment allows us to be balanced, posed and connected with Divine Reality.

Nothing in nature is ever still or static. God is an ageless, changeless pool of potential, yet God is expressed as creative thought taking action; for God to express there must be change. God changes into God.

We resist change because of fear. We fear our ability to handle the unknown. If we check in each moment, asking what is needed now – what must we do to express God – we know just the perfect action to take. As we stay in the moment, knowing it is God in action, there is nothing to fear. What can ever go wrong? God makes no mistakes. There are no errors in Spirit. God is in charge, creating God.

## Thoughts About Change

*Tammy L. Young*

In so many ways, change is a good thing. In many other ways, change is uncomfortable, scary, and intimidating.

Change is one way for us to make room for a greater good to evolve into our experience. Such is the case as in leaving a job. Sometimes we have to leave one place of employment in order to make room for a greater financial experience. It seems uncomfortable at times, however, we must remind ourselves that our greater good is already manifesting.

Change also means we must have an ending. Typically, there is a goodbye inherent in change. Sometimes, such as when we trade in a car, as I once did when I exchanged my sports car for a minivan, it does not seem to be a significant life change. However, sometimes these small changes can teach us a great deal about change in general and can demonstrate the resistance we all have toward it. I loved my Cougar. I had a deep emotional attachment to that car. Now it seems incredibly silly to me, but it was true. I had always felt that this particular car was a gift from God. The car and I had a partnership. I appreciated every day with that car. It felt like a pair of jeans. It just fit me. I planned to keep it forever. I never entertained the possibility that I would part company with it. We had been together for years.

However, the sports car started having some mechanical problems I had not been able to resolve. Also, my three children were getting bigger and were beginning to be pretty cramped in the sports car. The end result was that I chose a minivan, and my sports car is no longer my partner.

As I collected my belongings from the sports car, I cried. When I think back on that car, I sometimes still feel as though my dog has died. This was a painful goodbye for me. My first inclination was to criticize myself for such foolish emotion. However, I realized there was a valuable lesson for me here. I realized that my reaction was less about the sports car than it appeared. The whole process was more about change.

When I bought the sports car, I had an intention to keep it for a long time. I became attached to that intention as well as to the car. This had been a pattern in my life with things both big and small. I had always been a planner. Back then, I would plan every moment of the rest of my life if God had cooperated with me. Though I have made much progress in this area, it sometimes still shows up as with the car.

Change, faith, and surrender go hand-in-hand. Being fully present in the moment means that we must surrender our need to plan rigidly. We must be open to change at any moment. We must learn to welcome change. If we surrender our lives completely to the flow of Spirit in, through, and as ourselves, then we must surrender the need to know how it will all turn out. We must surrender the need to know exactly what tomorrow will bring.

Change involves endings, neutrality, and beginnings. New beginnings can be refreshing and exciting. To hold on to conditions and experiences is to deny ourselves the excitement of a new beginning, of a greater good in our lives. We must learn to say our good-byes with the assurance that a greater good is being manifest in our lives and with expectancy. Just as I had to say goodbye to my sports car, knowing that what was to follow would bring me even greater joy and satisfaction.

When we become grateful for opportunities to realize how we can be more open to receive the gifts that Spirit has in store for us through change, the realization that we must part with the lesser to receive the greater becomes timely.

If we can know for ourselves that all change is the natural evolution of Spirit in creation, then we can also know it for others. We can help ourselves and others see past the painful goodbyes and know the Spiritual Truth. That Truth is that behind every goodbye, there is a beautiful hello. In every transition, there is a potential butterfly ready to come out of its cocoon. We do not need to anticipate the outcome for ourselves or others. We do not need to know what color the butterfly might be. We only need to know that Spirit is expressing and evolving in and through every change.

## PRAYER TREATMENT

*Recognition:*

There is one loving, peaceful Presence in the Universe. This Presence is Spirit or God. God is omnipresent, omniscient, and omnipotent. God is the source and sustainer of all life. God is all there is.

*Unification:*

God is the creator and sustainer of my life right now. I am a spiritual being, one with God, one with all there is. The Presence of Spirit is at the center of my being in every moment. The essence of who I am is Love and Peace.

*Realization:*

I know that in this very moment, the creative, loving, peaceful Creator and Sustainer of my being is creating and sustaining every aspect of my life. Everything in my life is here by Divine Appointment. There are no accidents. I know that I am guided by Spirit to accomplish all things in the perfect time. In Spirit, there are no deadlines. My life is filled with peace and love. I love what is before me to do and I do it in peace. I release any anxiety about having things be "done" and I remain ever-present in the moment. I enjoy every moment to its fullest without regard to what the next moment might bring. I am filled with peace and I allow this peace to permeate every moment.

*Thanksgiving:*

I am grateful for this awareness. I am filled with thanksgiving for the peace and beauty of my life.

*Release:*

I release these words now into the Law of Cause and Effect, knowing that they are already manifest. And so I let it be. Amen

## Change
*Barbara Fox*

As a matter of rearing and habit, I learned to fear change. When I was a child, I viewed change as the enemy. I really cannot say what exactly caused me to instill such a strong feeling toward such a natural part of life, but I realize the beliefs I picked up during childhood surrounding change have been largely responsible for the discomfort I previously experienced during times of change.

Although I know I was molested as a child and that a large part of my psychological make up was tied to this, my childhood memories are hazy and often I find no tangible connection to the beliefs about change I once held and their inception.

My spiritual studies have shown me a way to facilitate change for my greatest benefit. One of the most basic things is simply to give myself permission: to allow new thoughts, ideas and beliefs into my consciousness. This requires a willingness to change on my part. The comforting part of this is I do not have to choreograph my development (thank God!); I simply must give voice to the desire to change for my highest and best good. I know this is true. I have seen it work in my own life.

As I look in retrospect at my early years in Overeaters Anonymous, I had no idea what needed to be changed or how to do it. I simply knew what I was doing was no longer working. Now I know that such a knowing is enough to bring about change in any desired area. People and things have appeared in my life to enrich my new, chosen path. Change was happening, and it continues to this day.

I wish I could say that's where the story ends, but this is not the case. Recently, I stumbled across a limiting belief I didn't even realize I held. Simply stated, I had held the belief that God leaves me just before things "go bad" and that He doesn't return until after they get better. Once I recognized I held this belief, it made sense to me why I was in so much fear and terror regarding a possible change in my career. Based on my unconscious beliefs, I thought I was going to have to do it all myself. In my limiting system of thought, God wouldn't be back to help until after I got things back on track, and since I had no inkling as to how I was going to do that, I was in deep trouble!

Based on the spiritual beliefs I now have which have served me, I was able to see a way out of this self-defeating spiral. Since I have had repeated success with simply having the willingness to change in areas of great need, I now realize that it is not necessary for me to know how to change things. It is enough for me to simply realize I need a change in consciousness.

My first step in this process is expressing my willingness to have my beliefs changed. My second step is to do prayer treatment and know in my mind that on the spirit level they are changed. Then form will follow thought as my new belief now unfolds into manifestation. I believe that these are the keys to enable me to consciously embrace change first in thought, then in outer life.

**PRAYER TREATMENT**

### *Recognition:*

Heavenly Father/Mother God, I know that you are All There Is. I know that God is the air I breathe, the words I speak, the incense that burns in my study. God is the love I feel toward my dogs, my family friends and loved ones. God is the thoughts I think. God is perfect, whole and complete. God is radiant health, divine order, lavish abundance, majestic and simple beauty.

### *Unification:*

Since God is All There Is, and because I am, I know that I live, move and have my being in God. I am a microcosm of the macrocosm of God. Just as God is, I am. I am and individualized expression of God's perfection, wholeness, completeness, radiant health, love, divine order, lavish abundance and beauty.

***Realization:***

And so I realize with a glad and comforted heart that my life is in divine order. It is a thing of grace. It simply must be as an aspect of God! I am lovingly guided to make healthy choices for my highest good. Change is divinely inspired and I see God in all aspects of my life. I am free of fear because I know God is my Source. I face my upcoming change issues with a calm expectancy of good, for God is always lavishly abundant and guiding me toward greater and greater heights. Only good can come to me! It is the way of God! I embrace these words and recognize them as the truth of my being.

***Thanksgiving:***

I am so thankful for these teachings that enlighten me and show me who I really am. I am grateful to know that that which I speak is already manifest in the mind of God.

***Release:***

And so I release these words to Spirit, with the calm knowing that they cannot return to me void. And so it is. And so I let it *be.* Amen.

# SECTION TWO

# *Creativity*

*"We share responsibility for creating the external world by projecting either a spirit of light or a spirit of shadow on that which is 'other' than us."*

– Parker J. Palmer

## Understanding How the Law of Creativity Works
*"Happy" Shaw*

The word *create* is a verb and to me it means the act of bringing forth something that was not seen before, such as a new novel, or something not seen in its present form, such as using pictures cut from a magazine to create a collage. However, our bodies also create new cells all the time just as the Universe creates new stars. So the word *create* is not limited to art or written work. In fact, the action of creating can be applied to almost any type of work or thinking because we make things and create situations in our interactions with people and with ourselves. It is hard to come up with any kind of situation where we could claim the act of creating is not present. Even rocks have molecules that are moving at a very slow speed, but which maintain the form of the rock.

The word *creative,* and adjective, applies to a person or something that creates forms or solves problems through thinking. We always talk about humans being creative, but elephants and cats both paint. So they are creative too. They also come up with interesting ways to protect their young and that is problem solving. So that is creative too. Birds build nests of all types. Sometimes improvising with some of the oddest materials. So that is creative. I think all of Nature is creative, much more so than most people think.

It is also creative for human beings to manifest problems in their life because the same law is used to create wealth as to create lack of wealth. So both negative and positive uses of the law are creative.

*Creativity* is a noun and to me it refers to that quality within which we can call upon to create or make things or solve problems. Artistic creativity is latent in a lot of adults and teenagers due to shaming or overly critical comments by teachers and parents on an elementary child's artistic efforts. I have met people who have told me that they haven't been able to draw or sing since they were in elementary school due to this kind of criticism. They have taken this criticism inside themselves and fallen under the "I can't" syndrome. This is very sad to me, as being artistically creative adds a wonderful dimension to life. I like to open this gift for people again and I like to push people to create at a level they have not allowed themselves to previously. That is very rewarding.

Since I have taught art to people from kindergarten to 65 years of age, I know it is possible to teach anyone to draw a decent picture. I have also taught the physically and mentally handicapped, and in all cases, the students were able to access this natural well of creativity within themselves.

All of these words *create, creative,* and *creativity* are natural states of everything. The Spiritual law of creativity causes illness sometimes in people who wished to express artistic or other creative talents and the person was forced by parents or society or economics to chose work or a livelihood which was looked on as having more status or "success value." I once knew a doctor who was miserable being a doctor because what he really wanted to do was be a history professor. He was a good doctor and had a nice practice which made him lots of money and satisfied his parents, but he was a very unhappy man and in many ways emotionally disturbed because he was not expressing God in his unique way through his own desires.

## What Creative and Creativity Mean To Me
Barbara Fox

To me creativity is a celebration of the senses. My spiritual studies have taught me that everything comes from Spirit, and therefore, creating anything out of nothing is questionable. When I think about creativity, I understand it is the formless, plastic unseen Spiritual substance which receives the impress of our thoughts and goes on to manifest those thoughts into physical form.

Recently, I was treated to a Spiritual experience of a most wondrous kind. It has redefined my outlook on creativity. I was quite frustrated with the "holding pattern" I was in regarding my business. The loan had not yet come through, and I did not know where my money would be coming from. I was nervous about what appeared to be mounting debt, and I was premenstrual, to make matters even more intense. When I find myself going round and round in my head, writing is often the only antidote. I logged onto the internet and poured out an impassioned e-mail to a close friend. In it, I ranted and raved about my deepest fears and concerns and just "Let it all hang out." The joy of e-mail friends is that you can write them in exactly the tone you desire and they don't interrupt; they don't try to cheer you up, and they listen to everything.

As I wrote, I proposed the idea to my friend as to what the self-actualized life would look like to me. Immediately my mood and my writing style began to change. I spoke of creativity as the key element in this life. This self-actualized life would be a place where the senses were showcased and celebrated in all their glory. I described my creative life as one where spiritual beings have a truly human experience. My surroundings would be filled with all the creative expression that is currently trapped within me. Each action would be a prayer. Sitting down to tea, stimulating conversation, decorating, entertaining, would all be nourishing experiences. By allowing the creativity in my heart to pour

## got spirit?

outward, I would in turn be awash in an atmosphere of joy, self-discovery and self-acceptance which would prove to be wholly contagious to all that enter the doors of my home. In this way, I would become a messenger of the Loving Source. People would visit me and instantly feel the energy; they would be drawn to listen to the still small voice, and their own gifts would be catalyzed into form.

This writing left me blessed with the gift of a personal epiphany. I saw quite clearly how creativity was the purpose of my existence. Small surprise that a creative act (writing) brought me to this understanding. Later, as I animatedly discussed my feelings with another friend, it was readily apparent to him I had found my purpose.

My recording voice work was but a part of this life. However, my whole life was about genuineness, authenticity, and true creative expression of self above all else. My male friend affirmed the life I described was indeed possible, likely, and perhaps unavoidable! I meditated effortlessly after that and later fell into a deep sleep.

For me, creativity means the expression of the impulses within me without judgment or suppression. This open attitude leads me to a greater and greater spiritual calm. This in turn allows me to feel more and more genuine excitement as further ideas well up inside me. To create is to breathe the Spirit essence through all my senses and watch, listen, taste, touch, smell and hear their exhalations. My seemingly most mundane experiences now have a magical reverent quality about them, and my more "formal" creative projects are no longer intimidating. This was a most inspiring awakening for me. I feel as though I have been given a priceless gift.

## Thoughts on Creativity
*Dave Schultz*

The terms "create" and "creativity" have, until recently, been associated more with the arts and literature for me. I think my upbringing had a lot to do with that view (big insight, huh?!?). I doubt if the terms "create" or "creating" were even part of my vocabulary during my early years and even through college. I grew up in a dairy farming community, went to one-room schools, attended a small high school, and then went on to engineering college. "Creating" seemed to have little place in milking cows, learning the three "R's," and solving engineering problems. The "creative" world was left to writers, artists, musicians and actors.

I learned to follow the rules, the scientific laws, the processes, the conventions and the prescribed and proven paths others had laid out. Everything worked just fine that way, for a long while. Life seemed to sail along by itself, events "just happened" to me, and I reacted according to formulas I knew well. I had no idea that I was already "creating" my life experiences.

During my second marriage, I began to understand that certain situations kept recurring in my life and that I had some responsibility in their existence. Through some excellent psychotherapy, I saw how I was contributing to difficulties I was experiencing. I learned that I could create and attract situations into my life. That was a breakthrough for me, but it was only the beginning of my understanding of "creating." The biggest pieces of the puzzle came through my Spiritual studies.

I learned three (I usually think in "threes") key elements about "creating" in my life. First, I learned about the power of thought as the initiator of creating. Secondly, I learned we are *always* creating with our thoughts, and thirdly, I learned that possibilities for creating my life experiences are limited only by my imagination and courage.

## got spirit?

Through studying Judge Thomas Toward's work, I learned there is a spiritual prototype, an essential being, of every existing thing. The material form of the thing that we see is the outward expression of it. So, when we make intelligent use of our mind, we create a nucleus of a thing which begins attracting material of like character. This continues until the thing actually materializes in this plane. This process works for everything – material things, life situations, feelings, other people, everything!

Not only can we intentionally create by using our minds, the scary thing is we are *always creating by using our minds*, consciously or unconsciously. "Oh, so that's how stuff shows up in my life that I think I don't want."

I'm unconsciously attracting it. I used to tell the students in my classes that a person cannot choose whether or not to model behavior; a person can only choose which behavior o model. The same is true of creating life. I cannot choose whether or not to create stuff with my mind; I can only choose which things I create. The principle is always working. The truth really is that the Universe only says, "Yes."

The third key element I learned is I can create for myself whatever I can imagine, and it will be done for me "as I believe." I believe in the concept and practice of "getting out of my box," but still find I tend to define my life possibilities largely in terms of what I've experienced up to now. How deeply ingrained in every cell are concepts of who we define ourselves to be, and I appreciate how that manifests in the world. Fifty years of programming requires unlearning and frequent mini-leaps of faith to change in my significant way. I'm working on those life lessons, too.

So, I am a creative being. I create continually and I am continually being recreated. I am a manifested creation of thought originated by my ancestors, made out of the stuff of the Universe, and recreated by my own thoughts and beliefs. The extent of my personal creativity is unlimited. I only need to choose to believe that.

## Create, Creative and Creativity
*Jeannie Bullard*

I am alive. I am a conscious, spiritual being. Inherent in consciousness is limitless creativity. As a conscious being, I must be conscious of something to know myself. At the instant of self-knowingness, I become a co-creator with Universal Mind. Created in the image of an infinite Creator, held as a thought within the eternal One Mind, I embody all the creativity of the cosmos.

To be creative, I do not need to do anything for it is a state of being. It is the quality of my spiritual channel. Originally and purely fashioned by Spirit and embellished by my experiences of self and the world, my consciousness shapes and molds the malleable flow of eternal spiritual substance. I share in an inexhaustible flow. I am spontaneous, self-creative expression.

I realize I have created everything in my world. Through the causation of my own thinking, I have drawn to me or manifested the out-picturing of my mind energy. I have clothed myself with the fabric of my intentions and perceptions. No other person views reality as I do.

My world consists of Inner States and Outer Events. That is all. My involvement with the outer world is DOING. My involvement with the inner world is BEING. Doing and being constitute the entire creative experience. Being organizes and aligns the energy and substance of the All and it springs into manifestation according to my energetic blueprints, the outline of my thoughts.

The creative process taught to me from the human viewpoint – "decide what you want, work really hard, do as much as you can and eventually you will have or be what you want" – is the Truth reversed. I now know that I must first BE and then the entire cosmos aligns so that I AM. The secret of all things is to BE.

Being *creativity* itself initiates the flow of change, of growth, of transforming patterns. It is interaction with life. It is all about relationship. Relationship to self, others, the world and the highest power, as I become more, I am the creator of more. I am the source of all that I choose to experience in life. Embracing personal responsibility for my world enhances my creative capacity. All proceeds from within. Creation flows outward from my inner world from my beingness. Creation is alive in me. Creating freshly and newly each moment. Artistically shaped by my unique view. I am a bridge passing divine energy from one state to another.

## PRAYER TREATMENT
### Barbara Fox

***Recognition:***

There is only one Power in the Universe. It is the Power in the Universe, of the Universe and through the Universe. This Power is the Loving Source, which I may choose to call "God." The Loving Source is an all-pervasive essence that is the substance of all things which exist, and all things which do not exist. The Loving Source is all things, emotions, behaviors, ideas, and actions. By Its very design, the Loving Source is infinitely giving, unceasingly creative, limitless in scope and possibility, unending energy, perfect order and divine.

***Unification:***

I know that I am one with this Loving Source. I am the Loving Source, expressing as me, demonstrating all its attributes as the unique expression as myself. I also know that this is true of _Insert Name._ _Name_ is the Loving Source expressing as _Name,_ and as such he/she possesses all the qualities of the Loving Source as this microcosm of the macrocosm.

It is with a glad and joyous heart that I declare, affirm, and speak my work for _Name,_ the Divine unique expression of the Loving Source. I declare that the truth of _Name's_ being is forever expressing itself and _Name_ is divinely inspired toward the perfect creative expression of his/her self as the Loving Source. His/Her energy is boundless and limitless; he is vibrant and alive with the vitality of Spirit.

Eagerly he/she steps up to take his place as Life expressing and in doing so, he/she can only do his/her perfect work. With each thought, word and deed he/she senses the divinity in all he/she puts forward and is further energized by a conscious awareness of the One. His/her work is multifold. As he/she serves others, he/she serves Spirit and himself. This is how it must be. He/she is perfection walking, and he/she revels in the knowing that it is so.

**Thanksgiving:**

And I am so thankful to know the truth of *Name's* being; that he/she is this Divine child of Spirit, giving and receiving the gifts of the Loving Source simultaneously, and that he/she is an infinite well of givingness. It is with much gratitude that I express my thanks for the teachings that allow me to know this about *Name.*

**Release:**

As I speak these words for *Name,* I release them into the Universe, commanding the Law, knowing that my words are made manifest now. It is good and very good. And so it is. And so I let it be. Amen.

# SECTION THREE

## *How Prayer Treatment Works*

*"Ask, and it shall be given to you; seek, and you shall find; knock and it shall be opened to you."*

– Jesus, St. Matthew 7:7

## MIND-BODY CONNECTION
*Lynne Curtis*

Think of the mind as being an ocean. The ocean has a surface and depths. We can learn the surface, map its bays and inlets and observe the calm and rough waters. But beneath the surface are vast impenetrable depths, full of mystery. It is difficult to see the mass of living things that swim there. We cannot tell where the surface ends and the depths begin. Storms only stir up a few fathoms of the surface while underneath the depths lie undisturbed and silent.

But there is only one ocean, not two despite my description. It is an indivisible one. Like the ocean, the mind is an indivisible one, yet has two distinctly different types of activities that take place in it. Our inability to grasp the different functions of those two aspects of mind can cause us great pain and difficulty. If you can understand the difference you can change your experience to bring healing and prosperity.

*Surface mind* is what Ernest Holmes in the *Science of Mind* textbook calls *conscious mind* or *objective mind*. This aspect of mind is what we use to dial a telephone number, play the piano or watch a movie. Surface mind directs the piano practice and playing of each note until, through repetition, one becomes so familiar with the technique of the individual finger movements that it actually passes into deeper mind and we no longer need to look at our fingers. This leaves the surface mind free to read the score, sing it or even carry on a conversation. Therefore, surface mind can also be called "directing mind" or the "I choose" mind. With it we weigh values, reasons for and against, we judge, decide, choose what we want to do, be or have. All our choices are made in surface mind.

*Deeper Mind* is the creating, the manufacturing phase of mind that takes what surface gives it and turns thoughts into things. It works ceaselessly to turn our thoughts – both good and bad –

into the outward conditions of our lives. It has no power of choice. It never reasons. It cannot refuse to take what surface mind gives it. It must always work from a pattern just like the soil must accept whatever seed is planted.

*Deeper mind* is habitual mind. Whatever we entertain often enough and vividly enough in our surface mind, whether by conscious, deliberate choice or by choice made so rapidly that we are not aware we have made it, that thought eventually passes into the deeper mind, where I continues to operate automatically. This is the process by which we learn everything that we learn. A negative disposition, for instance, is the result of repeated negative thought that has sunk into deeper mind and has become habitual. A happy, cheerful disposition can become just as automatic by placing positive thought into deeper mind. Deeper mind is the most reliable agent in the world for bringing choice into form. We can raise the level of thought of deeper mind by using the power of conscious deliberate choice that we have in surface mind. Deeper mind has access to limitless resources. It knows how to heal any condition, effortlessly. To it, there is no big, little, hard, easy.

ALL HEALING – WHETHER OF BODY OR AFFAIRS – ALL SUCCESS, ALL PROSPERITY, ALL MASTERY OVER DESTRUCTIVE HABITS, IS PRODUCED WITHIN DEEPER MIND BEFORE APPEARING IN OUTER MANIFESTATION!

Deeper mind keeps our heart beating, our lungs breathing, our food digesting, all without any conscious effort of surface mind. It carries on all the many and varied activities within our bodies that most of us don't even know about.

Why do people get sick even if in the present they fill themselves with positive thoughts consciously? A person may have a conscious experience today, tomorrow or next year, but he will have forgotten it. Yet it has not gone away but has merely passed from surface mind to deeper mind where it is stored for future reference. Every experience we have ever had does this. "Memory" or "recollection" is merely the recall of the surface mind of something that has been stored in deeper mind. This is why negative or destructive thoughts in due time will yield some experience that corresponds to them. We may think that it is unfair or mysterious but we are only reaping what we have sown sometime before. They don't need to bother us forever, as we can neutralize them by deliberate choice for the good.

Deeper mind is also the storehouse of the racial knowledge. It carries all racial consciousness in its memory. This human race consciousness exists and can profoundly affect our experiences. For example, smokers may say that they don't care about the risk of cancer and enjoy smoking, but their deeper mind takes in all the statistics and constant barrage by the media of its dangers

Deeper mind is characterized by the complete, unswerving obedience to surface mind. It has no power to choose; it can only obey. All its vast knowledge and creative power are dedicated to the person who learns how to use it. The vast creative force operating in our deeper mind is willing to make us whole. It knows only to obey.

To weave a rug you need a loom, threads and a weaver. The loom has one task, to facilitate weaving. The weaver may be displeased and outraged by what he sees coming out but he does not berate the loom and say, "Why have you done this to me?" He doesn't sit at the end and cry over the ugly pattern, wishing it would somehow change into a thing of beauty. He knows that to change the ugliness he must change the threads on the rack of spools before the obedient weaving apparatus gets the threads. He must take off the dark, ugly spools and replace them with brighter colors. The loom doesn't care what is fed into it. It is impersonal, just as the river doesn't drown a person who falls into the water because he or she can't swim. The pattern is set by the weaver and he is responsible for the result.

Daily, man's loom of mind weaves the pattern of his life. It is silly for him to complain about luck, providence, karma or fate.

Using intelligence, he must alter harsh, critical, unforgiving attitudes with more tolerant, kind, gentle ones. The loom is not against the weaver. He must gain the conviction that his deeper mind is the loom that momentarily weaves the threads of thought into the stuff of his outer world, and that the loom is always dependable, never dropping a thread of thought, but weaving ceaselessly whatever is given to it.

In summary, deeper mind is the working producing phase of mind, while surface mind is the choosing, selecting phase of mind. Surface mind chooses what shall come into the life, but is helpless to produce it. Deeper mind is the only agent in the universe that can bring that choice into manifestation.

## How Prayer Treatment Works
*Jeannie Bullard*

Einstein's famous equation $E=mc^2$ proved energy and matter are dual expressions of the same Universal Substance. This Universal Substance is a primal vibratory energy of which everything is composed. Einstein's scientific studies supported the great mystics before him – all energy is a form of light, and matter is this energetic light slowed to different vibratory speeds.

We are indeed beings of light in constant flowing motion – not solid matter. Matter is only an appearance of slowed light. Hermes Trismegistus and his hermetic philosophy of ancient Egypt and Greece taught that we exist in a mental universe and everything is energy vibration and by aligning ourselves with pure mind energy we can transmute the energy up the scale of vibration to bring about a higher correspondence of good.

My favorite scientific theory is that the entire Universe, including our bodies, is holograms. One pure light (Universal Mind) splits into two beams, one is reflected from the top down and the other is reflected to cast an image from the side. Where the two beams of light meet, an interference pattern, which slows and changes the vibration of this light, creates our visible bodies. The top beam is pure consciousness and the side beam carries a divine pattern of DNA to create form.

The three dimensional hologram of our bodies or the Universe is not a static display, but rather like a video with the action of all subtle energy fields acting upon it to create movement or change. Our bodies and the Universe are like a hologram in that the smallest piece of the hologram includes the entire oneness of the whole. UNITY – every piece contains the whole. The coronal discharge of the etheric and aura bodies are our holographic, energetic bodies that form a pattern for slowed light. Any application of energy into this energy system changes its vibratory relationship.

## got spirit?

Energy is introduced into this system through the power of mind or consciousness affecting vibrations up or down the scale. This change can be influenced by Divine or human thought. This explains the power of prayer, meditation, and treatment – the power to heal. Recent scientific studies have shown that pure light can be slowed, almost crystallized to produce a visible result – matter. All matter is frozen light. Packets of light, which mind can act upon by conscious direction into the system, changing its vibration.

The scientific now supports the mystical knowledge of the ages. Solid matter is an illusion; it does not exist. The light and love of Universal Mind is all there is.

**got spirit?**

## Using Spiritual Mind Treatment for Healing
*Rebecca Allen*

Recently, I have come to think of Spiritual Law as a sort of force field of energy. When we give a Spiritual Mind Treatment, we are entraining with the high vibration of Spirit and focusing the force field of energy like a laser.

If we think of Spirit as all there is (which is correct) we may think of the force field of Spirit as having all the frequencies of light, all of the color spectrum. When we give a mind treatment, or praying affirmatively, we are focusing and intensifying the energy and thought to the highest level.

Deepak Chopra writes about the field of all possibilities. There are vast, unlimited possibilities all around us. What we focus on is what we create; our focus is only trained on one item in a huge, universal possibility of creation. It is as if we turn our light – like a miner's helmet – onto only one small slice of the cosmic pie.

People, who are "suffering" from health issues, are down in a cave. They are seeing just a little of the light and that limited light is the chaos of white light, meaning just random firing of slowed energy. Their attention has become defused and chaotic, thus they have created a level of illness from their dark, limited perspective.

A practitioner of Spiritual Mind Treatment, affirmative prayer, sees a different frequency, the higher vibration. From the Infinite field of all possibilities, the practitioner sees health, vitality, energy and the highest good for the client. Turning on the laser light of Spirit's perfection, the practitioner illuminates another slice of the Cosmic Pie and the client's negative fields of vision fall into the darkness – and they see the *LIGHT.*

We now understand more about the entrainment of energy; we now know that thoughts actually are energetic. They are much like little photons of energy. Photons of energy can fire at random or we can get them to fire in unison – like a laser. A practitioner, by using clear, positive thoughts, may actually be causing thoughts to fire in unison with Spirit.

Thinking of our level of consciousness as a wave spectrum of light, then we must move our thoughts from the slow red frequency up to the faster violet or perhaps, the ultra-violet spectrum.

I think just the idea of asking for a Spiritual Mind Treatment or Prayer Treatment opens the client to the possibility of healing, it opens the mind to a broader field of possibilities. Simply asking for a Spiritual Mind Treatment allows the client a degree of focus which begins immediately to lift their state of awareness, or raise the vibration of their thoughts.

Furthermore, I believe a Spiritual Mind Treatment in the presence of a practitioner is especially powerful because, I believe, there is the additional entrainment benefit. In other words, as a client is in the presence of the practitioner, their thoughts become more focused and began to rise to the higher level, joining Spirit "in the field of unlimited possibilities" as Chopra would say.

Illness or "disease" is caused, I believe, because of chaotic thinking. We might imagine the thoughts. or brain waves or little thought photons are firing in chaotic or random order. That tends to create a field of dissonance or discord throughout our body. The light field begins to fire in chaos and disharmony, much like an orchestra which is out of sync or out of tune. In the body, this little organ. that little hormone, gets caught in the vibrational back-wash and gets slapped around by the disruption.

Perhaps we can think of the practitioner as a conductor bringing harmony and unison back to the orchestra. The conductor does not create or compose the music, nor does the conductor play the music, he/she takes the high view, and hears the parts as a whole. The practitioner does not create the healing. nor does he/she swallow the medicine – he/she takes the high watch and knows the harmony, sees the whole rather than the parts.

However, we can know the symphony is beautiful yet sometimes the music is played by a fifth-grade orchestra. It is up to the practitioner to hear the symphony, no matter how inept the musician.

### PRAYER TREATMENT

*Purpose:*

To appreciate and insure the continued strength and good health of my body, mind and spirit.

*Desired Outcome:*

A strong, healthy body, a sharp clear mind and a deep awareness of my connection with Spirit.

*Recognition:*

I know God is all there is. I know there is One Life. I know the One, which I call God, lives moves and has Its Being in all things. I know God animates and energizes all things seen and all things unseen – all things thought and dreamed - all things imagined and all things yet to be imagined. All is God and All is Good.

*Unification:*

Because I am one part of the universe, I know God lives, moves and has Its Being in me. I know the One Life is my Life now. I know God animates and energizes all aspects of my life.

*Realization:*

I open my mind, body and spirit to the outpouring of Divine Energy. I know that as I allow God's Energy to flow into my life, I am strengthened, energized and empowered. God's Energy heals what needs to be healed, clarifies what need clarity, energizes, vitalizes, empowers, stimulates, and motivates. With the strength of God working in, around and through my life and body, I know the harmonious action of Life now vitalizes all parts of my being and every area of my experience. I know my mind is clear, my body is strong and I am, at all times, fully aware that my personal energy source is my connection with Spirit.

*Thanksgiving:*

With the knowledge of God's perfect presence in all my

affairs, I give thanks. I allow Spirit to pour strength, vitality, health, joy, clarity and energy into every moment of my life, and I know it is good, and I give thanks.

***Release:***

With certainty, gratitude and faith, I have spoken my words into Law. I now accept perfect health, vitality, and clarity. I know I am always connected to the Divine Energy Source – and I now accept all the power, strength and vitality that I need from that Source. And so it is.

**got spirit?**

*My Notes About How Prayer Treatment Works*

# SECTION FOUR

# Intuition

"We have been given two ears and but a single mouth, in order that we may hear more and talk less."
– Zeno of Citium

## How I Use Intuition
*Barbara Fox*

My personal experiences as a sponsor in a Twelve-Step Program have brought the concept of intuition to life for me. When I first entered recovery, I became aware of the "white noise" in my head. As I gradually cleared my body of the excess food that was drugging me and clouding my awareness, I began to hear the still, small voice.

It was astounding at first – and quite scary. I didn't want to trust it. Gradually, through trial and error, I began to see the rewards of listening to it. When I followed my intuition, I invariably found myself in places of calmness and serenity like I had never known before. This became the litmus test for foreign experiences.

As I progressed in recovery and became a sponsor, I saw the importance of intuition in helping others. At first I was blunt, almost to the point of being abusive when it came to sharing what I saw in them. I had not yet cleared a path for gentleness toward myself. So I could not possibly be gentle with my "sponsees."

Then, as I became better versed in my own self-care, I began to hear the voice of my inner guidance as I sponsored others. My choice of words changed. Often the words came out of me without prior preparation. It was at that point I knew I was speaking the word of the Universal Mind expressing Itself as me. It is always an uplifting and delightful experience when this happens. It seems as though both myself and the person I am sponsoring sense the truth of what is being said. Expression of such a quality feeds back onto itself. Joy begets joy, and healing is inevitable.

The process of developing intuition is as important as water to the physical body. Without water, the body dies, just as the light of Spirit appears to dim without nourishment. This sustenance comes in the form of conscious contact with the Creator – through meditation, sitting in the stillness, or "practicing the presence" as Goldsmith said it. What we call it is not nearly as important as the consistent disciplined practice itself.

I trust my intuition to guide me to my greatest experiences.

### PRAYER TREATMENT
*"Happy" Shaw*

***Recognition:***

The Presence is always present. There is no time or distance in God's Knowing of Itself. It simply knows. And is.

***Unification:***

I am a part of the Presence who knows that this is true. My spirit is a self-knowing spirit. Time has no effect on this Truth. I am one with God and will continue to be one with God forever.

***Realization:***

God has been recognized and realized within me. There is no going back. I am here and God is here within me as me. I will continue to unfold my beauty as God expressed with each passing moment in each passing day. I am no longer afraid of losing that of which I have become aware. I cannot lose what I know. And I know. I radiate with this knowing of God's presence within me.

Because I wish to express even more of God and to expand my knowledge of knowing as much about God and Its relationship to the Universe as I can, I will continue my learning and studying because I cannot stop growing. This would be like asking a flower to halt in mid-bloom – an impossibility. God is always in the process of blooming and I, as God-recognized, expressing as me, can only do the same. Bloom, blossom and bloom again.

***Thanksgiving:***

I give thanks for knowing that it is impossible to close the door to God once we have realized that God is already inside us. I am filled with thanksgiving for discovering this Truth and for the spiritual unfolding that I am experiencing. I feel blessed, loved and whole – truly radiant.

## got spirit?

And so I give thanks for knowing who I am and where I am going and that my path leads ever toward blossoming spiritual growth and loving others and myself.

***Release:***

And so it is and so I let it be.

# SECTION FIVE

# *Faith*

*"Faith is a mental attitude, so inwardly embodied that the mind can no longer deny it."*
– Science of Mind Textbook Glossary

## Faith
*Rebecca Allen*

Faith is the engine that drives the universe. Faith is the thought which we put into the law; the "as you believe, it is done unto you." We all have deep abiding faith!

Each of us has faith in something. The trouble comes when we put our faith in the negative rather than the positive, when we believe in the disaster rather than the miracle, when we expect the bad rather than the good – and we are always right! We always get what we deep-down believe.

I think of my personal faith like a sandwich. The top layer – the surface – of my faith is the one where I freely declare: "God is good, there is only God and all is right with the world." The center of my faith is where the "scary-reds" live: "I'm not good enough; if I'm too happy, something terrible will happen." The center is where the fear and the petty little dramas lurk.

Underneath all of that, however, at the bottom layer, is a deep, abiding belief, a knowing, a "faith." Under it all, I know there is a core of me that is safe, untouchable and sacred. It is the place in me where God dwells. From that space I know only good will come to me. The sacred space, the space of faith, is the place where miracles are manufactured. At the very core of my being I remember my God connection, I remember love, peace, joy and harmony.

When I am able to stay connected and in touch. with my core, my God-self, then my faith is justified. As long as I hold to my spiritual center, life moves along smoothly, calmly and peacefully. The more faith I have in God's goodness, the more of God's goodness appears in my life.

Then, for some inexplicable reason, I allow myself to move into the scary-red zone. Inevitably, negative stuff looms up, casting huge, dark shadows across my path and my worst fears are confirmed (or, my faith in the negative is made manifest). Yet, even while I am in that space, there is a part of me which recognizes the shadows for what they are – illusions, smoke-puffs which have no substance.

Why do I do that to myself? I don't know. Why do some people ride roller-coasters or go to horror movies? Maybe I peek into the shadows to add drama to life. Maybe I need to create situations which force me to move deeper into my faith.

What I do notice is that I am finding myself spending less time playing around in that center layer of fear. The more aware I become of my God-connection, the more faith I have in the Divine process and the perfect unfoldment of the greater good, the less time I find myself hanging around with pain and melodrama.

As I develop a deeper connection with Spirit, my faith is proportionally developed. As my faith is developed, I find more evidence of God working in my life – which creates more faith.

I hope to soon integrate the superficial faith, the fears and the deep, knowing faith so there is never duality, never doubt and no mixed signals being sent out into the universe. When I have perfect belief, perfect knowing and perfect faith then I will have perfect demonstration.

## The Origin, Nature and Function of Faith
*"Happy" Shaw*

### Origin of Faith:

Beginning ideas about faith resulted in response to primitive man's contact with his environment. In primitive societies, when one fell over a rock, it was common to conclude that the rock had the power to cause harm. And if one possessed the rock and could use its power for one's own desires, then that was termed "good." The idea was then extended to using the rock's power against someone else in the tribe or against another tribe to gain whatever one wanted. Or using the rock or some other thing thought to have power as a gift to a god to get what one desired. So it is my understanding that the idea of having faith, its origins, came out of believing things outside of us had power.

Western traditional religious faith, in my opinion, does not go much further than the primitive man with the rock. Many religions teach that we must plead with a temperamental god to do our bidding by behaving in certain ways, placing offerings in plates or candles or prayer sticks at shrines or by saying a certain number of prayers in a certain way to gain favor. If we convince ourselves to have faith in our offerings being accepted by the god, then we believe the favor or request desired will be fulfilled by the god. The nature of faith grew out of fear and then was used as a way to obtain or use a power perceived as being outside ourselves.

I don't really like the word *faith* much, as it has too many old misconceptions attached to it, especially in my own history. Also, too many people put faith into things that are unworthy of their belief in them, and they are shattered when things don't happen as they had hoped or had faith in. Such as: the South having faith that their cause was a just one in the Civil War. People in the South were so emotionally shattered by having their faith destroyed that drug use in that area was tremendous after the war.

***Faith's Nature:***

When one has faith in something that will cause great harm to another, in the long run, the faith boomerangs on the first person, ultimately having a negative karmic effect. This kind of "faith" seems to always be motivated by fear or a sense of lack. I see what most of what the world terms as "faith" as nothing more than superstition, an unenlightened consciousness like that of people who continue to send out chain letters because they are afraid to "break the chain." Many people only pray or feel they need to have faith when a crisis occurs or they are confronted with possibly losing something or someone they value or have fears of the unknown. These people do not have a consciousness of a God who does not need to be placated. Even when these people express a belief in a god of love, they will still hedge their bets by sending the chain letter or whatever. Maybe even promising their god that they will quit smoking if the god comes through with whatever the person wants or is begging for.

I should know, for I fight this misguided, *learned* faith on my own path to spiritual awareness. I still find myself hedging my bets, doubting my faith in the God I express to believe in. However, I am becoming aware when I am slipping in to misguided faith, looking for a god *outside* myself or a duality that I know really doesn't exist. When a recent chain letter came to me, this time over my email on my computer, at first I felt fearful, falling into my old patterns of faith in duality. However, then I realized that if I have true faith in what I say I do and that I truly believe there is only God as I profess, and that God is All, then I could not send out the chain letter because that action would deny everything I now say I believe. I would be destroying my own faith.

***How Faith Functions:***

True faith is motivated from our God center and has Love behind it. If we are functioning totally out of fear, then that isn't really true faith. One of the most powerful images of faith in the

## got spirit?

modern era comes from a popular movie, "Indiana Jones and the Last Crusade." Most people just see the surface story, but this movie is grounded in the hero's journey myth as described by Joseph Campbell. The hero is very knowledgeable about ancient cultures' beliefs and practices of worship. He can *intellectually* figure out any puzzle presented him, using his book knowledge and previous experience. However, when he comes to the lion's mouth, a cave opening, leading onto a horrifyingly deep cavern that he must somehow get across to the other cave's mouth where the Holy Grail is supposed to be, the hero is at a complete loss. Nothing in his head is going to help now. And there is nothing in his environment – outside of himself – that he can use for help. His father has been shot and the hero must get across to save his father, who he dearly loves. All the hero can remember is a silly drawing of ancient people stepping out into thin air. The hero doesn't bargain with something outside himself to come and save him. Here, he knows if some miracle is going to be worked, it will somehow be worked *through* him. It is the hero's love for his father which causes him to step out into thin air, and when he does, he steps down onto a bridge, one that, until now, has been covered by an optical illusion. The hero's love for his father motivated him to have the faith he needed to accomplish this terrifying action.

On a metaphysical scale, it is our love for the Father of Creation, God or Spirit and knowing His love for us that allows us to step out onto the unseen support to fulfill the desires we have. A friend said to me, "God wants what you want and is not judgmental at all." That is a profound statement of faith.

I don't think the kind of faith displayed in the Indiana Jones movie is the same thing as what most people call *faith*. Or think of when they use the word *faith*. I think most people confuse hope with faith. Hope often is motivated by a feeling of lack. Where true faith finds its motivation in love, knowing that it is God's good pleasure (God's nature of Love) to give us the Kingdom.

## Faith: That Greater Awareness
*David F. Alexander*

When I think of Faith, I think of something that goes beyond belief. It is the strongest of beliefs. In faith, there are no doubts, no second guessing. Faith is pure and whole, unshakable. This is so because it is based and rooted in pure Spirit. If there is only one Law and that is the Law of God, which is the Law of Good. If there is only One Mind and One Power, then what is there to question? The Law cannot operate against Itself. Thus, all is acting and unfolding in the harmony of God. Right? Accepting and knowing this to be true is what faith is.

Many people have faith in things working out against their favor instead of for it, and they manifest experiences according to this faith. But if there is only one Law, how is this possible? Because the Law is impersonal and acts upon our thoughts without judgment. The fact is that as all things, faith works on a level of mental acceptance. Faith is a product of belief. So I have come to the realization that at all times in my life, whatever the level of belief I had about life, I also had complete faith in that belief no matter how flawed or incomplete it may have been. Therefore, as my spiritual conviction and understanding increases, so does my mold. As my mold increases, my consciousness meets it with complete faith in whatever system of belief may be in that mold at that particular time.

Sometimes our faith is discovered or strengthened by some event. Faith in my own life has been a very interesting process and evolution of greater understanding. I have found the deeper I have explored my spiritual side, the deeper my operation in faith has become. Faith for me is that greater awareness that there is something beyond and greater than I and that it is good.

Many people talk about faith as an all or nothing concept and I believe there is truth to such an argument. But this seems contradictory to the idea of my faith and spiritual conviction's deepening. For example, when my lung collapsed while on a guest speaking trip to St. Louis, I was more than shocked! As far as I was concerned, this health issue was in my past and I should not be experiencing it now of all places and time! Yet, moments after I had realized what was going on, I was overcome by a calm and peaceful state. That may sound strange considering I was still experiencing a great deal of physical pain. Despite all that, my faith had taken over the situation. My faith told me I would survive and that everything at this very moment (even in my struggle for breath) was perfect and in the hands of God. My faith saw me through! My faith was in knowing there was a greater power at the helm of the situation. I knew with complete conviction, I was a divine creation of God and despite appearances, I was expressing God to the Fullest. And so, my faith went beyond my physical expression and appearance to something intangible, yet I could feel Its presence. Faith is a trusting and knowing there is a spiritual universe with direct laws of operation which are exact and dependable. It has been through the deepening of my spiritual understanding that my conviction in the Law of the universe has become stronger.

I have always been intrigued by the many stories Jesus told about having the faith of a mustard seed. A seed when planted in the ground is acted upon by certain laws of nature. These laws are unshakable and impersonal. They follow a natural order and that never changes. The seed does not need to question these laws. It does not need to think about where it will get water, which direction is up, or how do I break out of this shell? It just does. There is no reason to distrust the law.

Human beings, of course, are not as lucky as the seed. We question what we know, we listen to other people and their opinions, we are affected by our environment and culture. I personally think we have a general tendency to make things much more complicated than they need be.

Faith is total acceptance of a greater power in our lives. Faith comes from our beliefs and our beliefs come from the culmination of all our experience. But that is only one part of faith. We also must not be limited in our faith. One must remember the Principle, which is what faith is based in – Spirit – is not bound by precedent. Knowing and trusting this is the ultimate demonstration of faith and conviction.

So, faith can help us ride out the storms and also help us find courage and strength in any situation;. Faith can also help us create the life that we desire. Our faith will manifest in our experiences.

On a practical day to day level, living in faith carries significant meaning to me. I believe the way to life in faith is to lead with your intention and not your fear. Fear is a lack of faith and I have reached a point where I am no longer willing to allow fear to guide my decisions. Instead, I believe in walking with my intention in front. This does not mean I ignore fear or hide from it, but rather I may embrace fear and allow my fear to be fully with me as I move forward anyway.

Here's an example, after returning from a church youth ski trip, I learned of a senior minister's death in another state. I felt an inner voice telling me I needed to be there for the funeral. Although I had several college papers due and a test to take that week, I decided to listen to the inner voice rather than the fear of not getting those assignments done. My intention was to listen to my heart and pay respects to a great man, whom I had had the privilege of knowing. I could have easily been held back by the fear of missing class and falling behind in school work. However, I had faith that all the details of my decision would work themselves out and that no harm could be derived from following my intuition. Indeed, that is exactly what I experienced.

While there, another minister was very touched by my decision to make the journey and he told me that he had not forgotten a previous conversation we had had and my vision of my work. He even went as far as to let me know that he felt that

## got spirit?

it was time for him to take me under his wing just as our deceased friend had done for him. Now there was no intention on my part to create such an outcome, but the result of following my heart exceedingly outweighed the cost of missing a few days of school.

As a student of and practitioner in tune with Spiritual laws, I believe it is my duty to walk in faith, lead with my intention and trust the ultimate process of good, and by doing so, inspire others to do the same.

## FAITH or *Haymanootha* (Aramaic)
*Jeannie Bullard*

**Sometime back, I defined Faith as:**

*Faith is a tool for re-connection. A safety line tethered to the Universal. Faith functions to mold my reality. It is the foundation upon which I build, my reflecting mirror. It directs my manifestations and demonstrates my mental approach to reality. Carefully cultivated mental habits comprise my basic beliefs, out picturing my faith. Faith is trust, either in things seen or unseen. It is an expectation of order, being and outcome. Faith is the emotional fire, the inspirational source that partners with will and desire to manifest my thoughts. Faith through its emotional nature is the all-important ingredient needed to arouse the dormant, latent or static. It gives rise to enthusiasm and positive belief. It is the foundation of my thought life. Without the ingredient of Faith, it would be impossible to manifest a desire. Faith is confident expectation. It is my inspirational vision.*

Through extensive reading, study, experience, I had defined Faith as something that could not be taught, but must be consciously generated, activated, expressed, cultivated, nurtured, convinced, and converted. I have applied these "actions" chasing after an illusive quality of faith. The more energy I applied trying to achieve a strong faith, the further I moved away from that attainment. I had been acknowledging that I did not have it – at least not in the form I desired – I bought into the belief that faith is something the "mind" must do. As if it were a kind of battle with duality – Faith vs. Non-faith. Just as there is only One Power not two, there is only Faith. It is a matter of degree.

My earlier philosophy of faith separated it as a tool, a companion, a function, an ingredient, a foundation, a mental practice, and a goal. It was a thing out there to attain and use. Now, I know faith is the original creative substance of man, and therefore, is man. I Am Faith. Faith is the original creative energy – It is *First Cause*, the power of creation. The Power that directs and initiates all creativity, all manifestation. This power is my natural inheritance. I cannot be without Faith. There is no exertion required. There is a simple releasing of the outer reality and a remembrance or returning to the perfect inner substance, the inner life, the inner knowing of I AM. Faith requires no struggle, no search, no work. Pursuing faith through actions only increases a belief in separation and duality. Faith is the original source, the purity of my expression.

I used to believe I shaped my faith through trial and error, as well as by the acceptance of (human) race consciousness. My faith was borrowed, personally proven or accepted – built upon the law of probabilities, averages and confident expectations, observation, experience.

My previous accepted picture of faith was very outer directed, very human. But, now my perspective is Divine. Faith is my Essence. My original Divine Pattern. Faith is the Word of God. The Power of One Mind, the Force of Life. The Energy of creation itself, It can never be depleted or diminished. But I allowed my small ego mind to make choices along with cultural expectations and race consciousness to encrust and obstruct the original light. But at the instance of revelation of this Truth, every obstruction falls away. My faith is that of a little child, no thought, no work, no struggle, just acceptance of what is.

I don't believe I have a choice not to have Faith. Faith is. I am Faith. What I can do as an independent, God-creation is look away. Deny the Truth. Through release and surrender I come home. It is the prodigal son returning, that illuminates the Truth. The great omnipotent Power of the One is Faith. God is Faith. I am made of God-substance. I am Faith.

I no longer use faith in my prayer treatments. Faith is. Faith is life. It is me. It is the client or friend, requesting a prayer treatment. It is the solution. It is the appearance of concern. It is the perfect outcome. When I find myself struggling, becoming involved in the appearance, of feeling I need to fix something, I recognize the need to release and to turn inward to the Source. The Source is All. The words spoken, the treatment, is the Energy of Faith/Spirit flowing through Itself. The treatment is complete. There is a Source for Good in the Universe, and I AM It. Faith is a synonym for God/Consciousness.

## Learning to Have Faith
*Tammy L. Young*

The reality is there is no such thing as having a little faith or a lot of faith, either you have faith or you do not. Faith is developed from an experimental approach to an inner knowing that comforts and reassures us daily. Sometimes we have lapses of memory where we seem to forget that all is well, but we can easily remind ourselves. Having faith can become as natural as breathing. Whenever considering a "problem" in life we can remind ourselves that we do not have to manipulate our way through the problem or find a way to avoid it. We can just know, in spite of all appearances, it really is not a problem at all. Whenever someone else shares "problems" with us, we can know that *everything* is, and will forever be, okay.

Sometimes it seems as though our lives are chaotic. This is especially true when we have a lot of obligations that seem to require more time than is available to us. However, we can feel ourselves centered as if in the eye of a hurricane. Though most of us have never actually had this physical experience, we can experience it in a mental state during those chaotic times. We can find that calm "eye" and remain centered there until the storm subsides. There is no danger putting ourselves mentally inside this calm eye, for wherever the eye goes, we also go. Wherever we are, Spirit is also.

We must learn to pay attention to the intuitive aspect of our being. We can set intentions that allow Spirit to take over. We can allow Spirit to create through us and joyfully take on the role of co-creator. Doing this affords us great peace. It removes the sense of burden that we may have once had, knowing that the Ultimate Intelligence of the Universe is our partner and together we will see this through. We can know that we are divinely guided, and we are able to ask the questions and not wrack our brains for answers. We can know that the answer will come. We can become much more open to opportunities because we will not discount

## got spirit?

anything that Spirit puts in front of us. We can practice having faith by repeating the phrase: I know when I know.

By developing faith, we can come to honor other people and situations to a degree that we have never even imagined. In our past, it might never have occurred to us to honor life the way having faith will cause us to now do. And honoring Life is reciprocal. If we honor Life, Life will honor us.

Where to start? If we are mothers or fathers, we can start by feeling honored to be the parents of our children. Or we might start by feeling honored to be someone's spouse or partner. We can feel honored to work with the people we find ourselves working with. We can feel honored to have all that we have in our lives. A sense of honor can be constantly welling up inside of us. After practicing honoring others by having faith that everything is perfect, we can often experience a state of amazement at the perfection of things. Some small event will send us whirling in amazement. We can sense Spirit in situations, in people, and in ourselves. It will be an awesome and humbling experience every time it happens.

Having faith allows us to have fewer attachments to outcomes. We can do less outlining. Of course, each time we fall back into outlining outcomes, we can reconnect with our faith and Spirit will then remind us that we need not outline anymore. Every time we have an attachment, we can eventually come to see that there is something better trying to emerge through the thickheadedness of our attachment thinking. Not having an attachment to the outcome will allow Spirit to unfold in the most beneficial way possible. When we get out of the way, the results are outstanding.

The unfoldment of life is always in consciousness, and with faith, we can come to see life as a blossoming flower. We can witness our own learning and growth in uncomfortable situations. We can create new beginnings out of endings. We can watch life unfolding and know that it is taking us to where we need to be and to where we want to be. Even when we do not understand, we can still know that we are being divinely guided.

With faith, relationships can become easier. We can start expecting less of other people and give more of ourselves – not in old co-dependent ways. We can do what we need to do to protect ourselves, but we can forgive others more easily. We can reach a place where we no longer need to prove that we are right. It can become less important to hear that someone else was wrong. We can remove ourselves from interactions that we do not like instead of engaging in non-productive conversation or activity. We can allow ourselves to walk away.

With faith, we can learn to be honest in different ways now and more honest with ourselves. With faith, we will know where we stand with ourselves and with others. We will no longer need to pretend to be enchanted when we are not, no longer need to pretend to think in a certain way, to feel a certain way, or to want a certain thing. With faith, we will learn to be authentic with others because we are authentic with ourselves.

With faith, we can allow ourselves to learn and not make excuses for ourselves or blame others. We can assess our choices and acknowledge when we wish we had done something differently. With faith, we no longer need to beat ourselves up. With faith, we will learn to deal with any "mistakes" and move on.

Living a life of faith allows us to have an increased level of commitment to ourselves and to express more of the true nature of our being. We can be conscious. We can be awake. We can be aware. We can put our best foot forward and know that we are a Divine expression of the One. We can *know that to be true*, and we can walk in that TRUTH.

With faith will come outward changes, but these are only a reflection of the inner work. It is not always easy to confront the things about ourselves that prevent us from drawing a greater good into our experience. It is sometimes painful to acknowledge that our choices have created our reality. It is occasionally frightening to go on. There is often a degree of discomfort in the realization that in order for things to change outwardly, we have to do more changing inwardly. The discomfort can be short-lived and we can overcome it on this journey. We can turn to the people we share this journey with who mean a lot to us. Those people who understand the meaning of the work that we are trying to do. There are people of courage like ourselves that we can connect with, but it is more important to acknowledge the courage within ourselves, for it does take courage to walk the path of faith.

However, with our ever growing faith, we can continue on to become a beacon of light. We must become that light for ourselves and all those around us. Our mission is to allow that light to shine in ourselves so brightly that it must touch those around us and help awaken them to their own light. We must be deeply committed to continue to allow Spirit to show us the way to do this, and if we do, some day soon everyone will recognize the perfection in each child of Spirit on this planet.

## PRAYER TREATMENT

### *Recognition:*
I know that there is One Life, One Love, One Divine Expression individualized in countless ways. I know that everywhere God is present as this Divine Expression. I know that there is one Divine Love, which orchestrates everything in the Universe. This Love is God. God is. God is all there is.

### *Unification:*
This Love is in me, through me, and all around me. I am an expression of the One Life. This life is my life. I am immersed in Divine Love. It permeates my every thought, my every emotion, my every idea, and every cell in my body. This love is the essence of who I am. I cannot be separated from Love, as I cannot be separated from God.

### *Realization:*
My life is an expression of love. I devote my life now to the

greater unfoldment of Divine Love in and through me. I surrender completely to that Love and allow it to be the driving force of my life. This Love guides me, protects me, and completes me. This Love works through me to give greater understanding to everyone everywhere about the Divine Nature of each and every one of us. This Love is without limitation and it heals every wound, dissolves all confusion, and opens every heart. I embody this Love completely. It is who I am. I express this love to every person I meet and I know Spirit works through me to accomplish great things. I give my life to this Love and I give this Love freely. The Power of this Love, through me, creates a greater awareness and a greater understanding for myself and for others.

### *Thanksgiving:*

I give thanks for the sense of purpose that permeates my being, for the Love, which is the very essence of who I am, for my life, and for my life's purpose. I graciously accept the abundance of love in every moment.

### *Release:*

I release these words now into the Law, knowing that they are spoken with Power and with Conviction. They cannot return to me void. And so it is and so I let it be. Amen.

# SECTION SIX

# Prosperity

*"It is the Father's good pleasure to give you the Kingdom."*
– Jesus, *New Testament*

## A Letter About Ego and Prosperity
*"Happy" Shaw*

Dear One,

When one has a dark night of the soul, it is so that one can emerge more fully into the light. Sounds like a lot of airy fairy crap, doesn't it? But look at it this way: Would you want to go to a spiritual practitioner, doctor, healer, or counselor of any kind, who did not have a clue as to what you were going through? Me neither. It is all grist for the spirit mill.

We all have these growing pains financially and spiritually. I have to laugh at myself sometimes as I pull pubic hair off the towels I just washed and dried at the B & B where I presently work and I chop up fruit for the guests' breakfast or I wash their dishes, knowing at the same time I just got selected for *Who's Who of American Women* and I just started my own publishing company. But frankly, both are just facets of where I happen to be in this present time in this particular body experience. I will soon be onto other experiences and these new ones will also fade into the past – if I let them – just as all experiences are supposed to do. Whether we label them as "good" or "bad" experiences.

Rev. Jac Blackman quotes of times like this, "And it came, (in order) to pass." To the Universe, they are just experiences. So what? No experience diminishes or increases who I AM, or who you are, for on a Spiritual level, we are both one and the same Spirit. We can't become any more spiritual than we already are, but we can chose to show it more.

And remember: Spirit is of the same strength at all times, whether my mind/body experience is being perceived by the little mind (or ego) as good or bad. It is my perception of the event(s) that shuts down my realization of the Spirit within me and of the positive possibilities embedded within the experience.

The stuff you are going through now is just the final healing step away from "victimhood."

## got spirit?

You will find out soon, that the free will thing is just a function of the little ego. Actually, no matter what we do, say or believe or in spite of any act or crime we commit or that has been committed against us or even any thought we think, we belong to Spirit and It will never give us up – no matter what. This is the key to everything, dearest, knowing that you are loved beyond measure. But I am sure you don't feel loved – because you do not let yourself be. Your ego wants to hold you in place.

It hates change. It is terrified that it will not exist anymore if you fully heal.

Dearest, quit finding excuses for not being good enough for anyone else or God. You've already lost the battle. God has created you out of Itself, as yourself, therefore, you must accept that who ever you are – even right now – however you are, no matter what state you are in – miserable, crampy, crabby, compassionate, loving, hateful, whatever, you are God in form. You might not be acting as if you know the Truth about yourself but that is okay too. You might as well accept it because it is the Truth no matter what your ego, little self, is whispering in your ear.

Ego can be as negative as positive, and yours is a lot like mine because we have traveled some of the same pot holes. Tell your ego to take a break, that you aren't listening to it any more because you know who you are.

All that is happening to you is that you are being asked by your Spiritual Self to give up some old thoughts and some old patterns and your ego is screaming that you can't have, be, do whatever you always dreamed. But the fact that you have dreamed it at all is the seed that God has planted inside of you and that Spirit is watering right now with your tears and now your reality of being is about to pop through the soil (darkness) and into the light of the Truth.

Heard something really interesting today at church and that basically was, there is nothing wrong with having money, but you need to know who you are before having it; otherwise having money makes you nuts as you worry about losing it.

## got spirit?

My conclusion being: it does not matter if you lose it because when you come to know you are Spirit you can attract it again and besides, "having money" is not who you are anyway. You are more than that. When we both learn the latter lesson, the money will fly to us like a magnet. And when we backslide in to old tapes or doubts and we lose our money, who cares?

Like the man that Jesus asked, "Do you want to be healed?" we can pick up our pallet and walk, again and again – if we need to. All Spirit asks is that we move forward toward perceiving It rather than the illusion of "other stuff." Then Spirit will rush toward you and me, showing us the Truth about ourselves that was there all the time.

I'm still learning all this stuff myself. And more. I fall on my face spiritually constantly. Who cares? As long as I pick myself up again.

Remember that we teach and counsel on that which we need to learn ourselves and just because we haven't learned it all yet, it does not mean that we cannot help others. Goes back to what I said in the beginning. At least we have a clue as to what people are feeling. If we didn't, we couldn't help others lift their pallets. Makes you wonder what Jesus must have gone through to become the teacher of all teachers, doesn't it? Oh, yeah, I think they called it a cross.

## PRAYER TREATMENT
*Rebecca Allen*

### Condition
I fear lack and depravation. I'm afraid I won't have enough money to meet my needs and usually I am short. I feel worthless and unworthy of good in my life.

### Desired Outcome
A life of service, comfortable prosperity and abundance.

### *Recognition:*
There is one Presence which is All. This Presence is limitless, enormous and abundant beyond measure. This Presence is All there is, It is in all things, seen and unseen. The Presence is the Unifying Force which creates the universe, is the universe and is ever expanding and creating all that is. This Presence is limitless and boundless, It knows no lack or restrictions. It is All. I call this Presence, God.

### *Unification:*
I am one with the Presence. I am one part of the entire whole of God which is the limitless Universe. Because God expresses generously, without stinginess or reservation, I know I have my full measure of the Divine Spirit expressing through me. Because God is all there is, I know that all I am is God, all I think is God thinking, and all I do, feel and believe is God in action.

### *Realization:*
Because I have my full measure of God, I know I lack nothing. I have all I need to be joyful. I know that God acts through me and expresses through me and gives me my own unique service and purpose.

I trust God to provide for me in unique and perfect ways which meet my every need. I know as I listen to God and act in God, my every desire comes to me with ease because they are God's desires.

I let all false beliefs of lack, depravation and unworthiness drift back into the mist of clouded thinking. Just as the sun breaks through the fog of dawn, Spirit shines through to illuminate the Truth, and when the fog is lifted, I clearly see the Perfection.

### *Thanksgiving:*

I have so much to be grateful for. I am grateful for the peace which comes with trusting my Divine connection. I give thanks for the clear knowing and the Divine expression of my higher purpose. And I give thanks for all joyful forms of abundance and prosperity which pour into my life for the good of all.

I give thanks for my personal beauty, purpose and meaning. I gratefully acknowledge and accept my higher purpose. I celebrate my unique talents and opportunities for service. I joyfully accept God's goodness which shows up in many forms of gifts, unexpected income, abundance and prosperity. I let my prosperity come to me now. I am grateful and I give thanks.

### *Release:*

I trust my word is openly received and acted upon by the Law. I release all my concerns and worries and I know God is acting in my life and it all is perfect. I let it be so, and so it is.

# SECTION SEVEN

## Integrity

*"Begin with the end in mind."*
– Stephen R. Covey

## Integrity
*Tammy L. Young*

The dictionary defines *integrity* as *"uprightness of character, honesty; quality of being unimpaired or sound."* The word means this and more to me. It means doing 110% in what I do, to be dependable and accountable, to hold myself to the highest of standards and to always be someone who goes above and beyond. Integrity, for me, means to be forthright, open and honest, to serve as an example – someone my peers can be proud to be associated with. I know that I expect a lot of myself and I have made an effort to consciously monitor whether or not my own expectations are realistic. By this I mean both the expectations that I hold for myself and for others. I have a tendency to expect others would also want to be the very best they can be. I have to remind myself at times that the choices I make for myself cannot be imposed on others. I have also learned that sometimes my enthusiasm can spread to the people around me and it's a win-win situation. As with everything, the more I concern myself with my own activities and state of being, the better off everything around me is.

### PRAYER TREATMENT

***Recognition:***

I know that there is one Loving Presence and Power in the Universe. This Presence is the Source of all Life. It sustains all Life. It is God. God is Love and Joy, Peace and Wisdom. God is omnipresent. God is the Life of all that is. God is all there is.

***Unification:***

I know that I live and breathe and have my being in the Presence of God. At the center of my being is pure Spirit. I am a part of the Ultimate Life and Love of the Universe. The life of God is my life. My essence is all that God is.

***Realization:***

I have a deep, abiding faith in the Power and Presence of Spirit in my life. I know that in all that I say and do, I am guided by that Spirit that exists within me. In everything I do, I know that I act with integrity. Divine Wisdom flows through me animating my every decision, my every intention, my every activity. I express my God-being and in every moment allow Spirit to be fully expressed through me. In every role I play in life, I know that my character emanates Love, Honesty, and Integrity. This is the truth of my being.

***Thanksgiving:***

I give thanks for this truth and for this awareness. I am deeply grateful for the many gifts in my life, for my spiritual journey, for my family and my friends, and for the absolute overflowing abundance of the Universe, I give thanks.

***Release:***

I release these words now knowing that they are received into the Law of Cause and Effect and cannot return to me void. And so it is!

**got spirit?**

*My Notes On Integrity In My Life*

# SECTION EIGHT

# *Death and Life*

*"The unexamined life is not worth living."*
– Socrates

## Abandon All Hope – A Love Story
*Lynne Curtis*

I am inviting you to entertain the idea that hope can actually keep us from our good; that it diverts our attention from the present moment and masks the richness of the *now*. I will ask you to abandon the hope of alternatives to this present moment, the hope that suffering and pain will go away, the hope that things will always remain the same, hope that insecurity will be exterminated, hope that we can always stand on solid ground, hope that there is some place, some person, some condition that lacks discord and challenge, hope that we can control the circumstances that arise in our lives. I will ask you to remember that bad is not a punishment and good is not a reward. I will remind you that just because there is suffering, it does not mean that something is wrong. I will ask you to consider that there may not be anything wrong with chaos!

What if things don't turn out the way we want them to? What if the person we have our expectations centered in disappoints us? What if, we believe God will fulfill our wishes and hopes and that doesn't happen?

I would like to share with you a personal story about hopes and dreams. A story of how I learned to abandon all hope and it proved to be the most significant experience of my life. It proved to be an incredible test of me and my commitment to an intention as well as an exercise in humility and grace.

However, first, I'd like to tell you a story about Trungpa Rinpoche. He is a Buddhist mystic who was visiting a monastery he was not familiar with. There was a ferocious dog tied up at the gate. The dog was desperately trying to get at Rinpoche and his attendants Eventually, the dog broke his chain and ran toward the visitors. All the attendants froze in terror. However, Rinpoche took off, running full speed toward the dog. It so startled the dog, that it put its tail between its legs and ran off.

## got spirit?

We all have a ferocious dog before us at times but rarely do we run head on into it. The ferocious dog is like our hope, a way of separating ourselves from our dramas so we won't have to deal with them. Its a way of waiting for some shuttle bus to arrive and free us from our circumstances.

I spent time with my ferocious dog for the better part of a year. It was the most tender yet completely unnerving experience of my life.

To begin my story, I need to go back to 1968. I was stationed at Oakknoll Naval hospital in Oakland, California. It was during the Vietnam crisis and I was assigned as the head nurse on the eye ward. One of the patients was a man who had been grievously injured when he elected to lay on a grenade rather than throw it and injure one of his men. He had already been a patient for 14 months and had undergone some 24 surgeries including his fourth corneal transplant which up until that time had been unsuccessful.

I didn't like him much at first, but over time, I came to respect and admire this man who never felt sorry for himself and continued to live like a hero an a daily basis. I was attracted to his vulnerability and honesty and we quickly developed a rich friendship. The circumstances under which we fell in love were fueled by the times; openness, "make love not war," and "peace brother!" It would be another corneal transplant – finally successful – several more operations and five years before we finally married. However, we had great hopes for our future. He even followed me to Brazil, not taking "no" for an answer, where we were married and honeymooned.

This was the first serious relationship I ever had or have had to date. I'd like to say that our relationship was blissful; however, the cracks began to show after only a few years. The truth is that the openness, vulnerability, intimacy and compassion we had for one another went underground, more and more every year. We really loved each other, but our egos got to be bigger than we were and we started looking for things that might make it better. We hoped that we would change, that the right counselor would show up, that we would find a better way to communicate or that somehow some magical thing would happen which would take us back to those wonderful times in the beginning.

We went to school, bought a house, had a child and did all the other things people do when they live together. However, in the end, we allowed the discord to grow bigger than we were and we divorced. There was so much anger and disappointment and even bitterness that if he wanted to talk to me he wrote me a letter. I made a few feeble attempts to communicate for the sake of our daughters, but the truth was that neither one of us wanted to give up our self-righteousness.

Years later, he became very ill and almost died after a surgery to lessen the effects of his emphysema. I think it was at that time I began exploring the possibility of healing our relationship and his brush with death was opening the door if ever so slightly. What I noticed was that we had been divorced for six years and neither of us had had another relationship. Perhaps, just perhaps, there was something we needed to complete.

His experiences had touched the soft spot in him, and I had been spending years exploring my own "soft spot." I made the intention to be open to healing if that was in our highest good. It would be another year before I really had the opportunity and it came in the guise of our needing to talk about our daughter.

In the fall of the year before, he had had a couple of hospital admissions to clear up a "stubborn pneumonia." I visited him daily and we began to talk for the first time in years. At Christmas, I asked him to attend the church dance with me, for I had gone alone for five years and I was tired of that. We had what proved to be his last real date that night.

In one of our conversations, I intuited that he really had lung cancer. However, I said nothing to him. At first, many of our conversations were guarded and stilted as we carefully chose our topics of conversation, but at least, we were talking. It was in the next few months that a ferocious dog appeared in the living room.

I began cooking his meals for him and taking them up to his house. We made a business arrangement about that. I took him to his doctor appointments when his daughter couldn't, and I spent time with him when she was out of town with her new husband. What I noticed first was the level of comfort we had with one another. There is something about knowing someone intimately for thirty years that just doesn't die when you get a divorce.

I held him as he mourned leaving his home, for he knew he would not be back. I sat with him when they suggested chemotherapy and radiation might be the best approach for this kind of cancer. It was so hard to look death in the face. At first, I so wanted to change it, to control it. In the early stages, we clutched at straws, trying this homeopathic, that medication, this machine or whatever popped into our heads. I was so uncomfortable with having to wait, being insecure, experiencing panic and feeling helpless and impermanent. I often wanted to bolt from the room and have this nightmare behind me. I wondered what was I thinking of when I got started in all of this! I hated the sand slipping between my fingers. I dreaded time, I hated *old*, I hated *sick*, I hated losing and I hated change. I wanted to be there all the time and I didn't want to be there at all.

As he slept, I would ponder the times I felt that marriage was good but divorce was better. That relationship was better than being alone. But I'd come to believe that being alone was better than trying to work out a tough relationship. That making love was better than having a friend, but now having him as a friend was better than having sex. That good health was better than illness, but now I was feeling that it is easier to heal in the face of cancer than to fix an unhappy marriage.

One day I was sitting with him and found myself compelled to look to my side. Before me was a picture so vivid and so real that I was startled at first. I saw a hallway in the house we had when we were married, and I could see him on one side of the hall. On the other side, I was standing. Between us was this great gray cloud which obscured our vision of one another. I knew it was the discord we had had in our marriage, and I could sense we had used it as our first line of defense against having to be intimate with one another. In the center of the cloud, coming from far away, was this luminous string of light which passed through the cloud and came into the hospital room. Then the string of light continued on into infinity. I could see that the string of light was Love, an unbroken stream of Love which had existed long before we did, which threaded through our experience here in the now and which continues into forever.

I felt stunned by this incredible insight. I could see that no matter how much we try to hide from the Light, Love is always there, waiting. I never told my ex-husband about my awake dream, but I could see that he knew of it anyway. In all those months together, never once did we talk of the discord we had once had in our marriage. Never once. It was amazing. All of the petty nothings we had thought were so important at the time had no real meaning. There was only now, this present moment, for he may not have tomorrow. So we didn't waste our time trying to massage our egos.

I realized that the vulnerable, open, sensitive man I had once fallen in love with and spent most of our marriage trying to find, had returned. Our defenses were dissolved. In this process, I felt myself begin to relax into the unknown. I began to abandon all hope. I realized my littleness, my powerlessness to control circumstances, and I felt humbled as I watched this man face his fears with incredible grace and dignity.

During those wonderful/awful days, I found it demanded a great deal of me to be there – willingness, yielding, devotion, rectification, apology, staying in the moment, support without caretaking, humor and humility among others.

## got spirit?

It also took abandoning all hope that I could be in charge. In doing so, I found the greatest gifts I have ever received. I was able to be there for the completion of our relationship. I felt whatever karmic intention we had forged together, it was complete. It was if a karmic membrane had ruptured and we were both now free to move on.

We were able to acknowledge each other and find that luminous stream of Love and connection that was there all the time but hidden behind a cloud of discord, arrogance and ego. We were able to experience our hearts, our largeness, our bravery and our compassion, and we were able to bring four estranged people to the beginning of a new possibility. I often blessed the cancer for ripping open our hearts and him for being willing to suffer it. So we could heal.

We discovered a Great Truth – that our present awareness contains the entire truth, that we are always looking right at the answer to our Great Search – that Spirit is present in our awareness right here, right now, fully, totally and completely.

## got spirit?

## Thoughts About Living and Dying
*Barbara Fox*

In my life, I have been shielded from death and dying. When my grandmother passed away in 1977 from leukemia (I was fourteen), I did not grieve. I did not cry. I didn't attend her service. When the family dog was put to sleep a year later, I was inconsolable. An adult relative's only comment was a sarcastic, disdainful, "You didn't even cry when you grandmother died and you're crying over a damn dog!" I learned right away that there were rules to my grieving, and I didn't know them but my relative did. Needless to say, death had its own built-in pitfalls for me. It was easier to avoid the subject than really give it my attention.

One summer day in 1995, I received a call. The caller informed me that her brother, a friend I had known since elementary school, had died of complications resulting from testicular cancer in December of the previous year. Like a textbook case from Elisabeth Kubler-Ross's *On Death and Dying*, I immediately went into denial, telling her how she must be mistaken. This was her brother she was talking about. She knew the score, but I was out of my head. After I got off the phone, I went into shock. How could this be? He was only thirty years old, and he had a one-month old son. My inner voice spoke loudly and clearly. I called another close friend back East and we concluded that I would have to go out there. We knew we needed to be together. It was a really big deal for me. I had never been allowed to just deal with my feelings surrounding a death prior to this. (There had been relatively few in my immediate circle of friends and family.)

As I was on the plane, my own life a mess with a dissolving marriage, I asked myself why I was on a plane going to see a grave. What good could it possibly serve? I really wasn't sure, but I just knew it needed to be. My mind raced with the significance of all the events of my life and the priorities they would eventually occupy. At the moment, they were just linear occurrences that had no rhyme or reason to my intellect. I just sucked it up and muddled through.

When I got to New Jersey, my deceased friend's mother picked me up and together we drove to the grave site. I fell to the ground and began to babble and weep. It was my turn to be really surprised. I came from a family where we did not cry or show negative emotion, and here I was with tears streaming down my face. My friend's mother was wonderful. She told me she was going to leave me to be by myself at the grave site. I sat there and just let the feelings flow – a very scary thing, since I didn't know where they would lead me. I might never stop crying. I might go hysterical. I was not comfortable with uncontrolled emotion, but this was nothing I could repress. It had to come up and out. There was no debating this. I continued to cry and talk to my deceased friend. As I did so, I remember thinking back to scenes in the movies where people would talk to a deceased relative or friend at a grave. It seemed so silly and schmaltzy to me at the time, and here I was doing that very thing, quite naturally. Eventually, the tears did come to an end, and together, my friend's mother and I left the cemetery.

As I returned home to my ambiguous marriage, I realized that I, too, had to accept a death of the relationship. I had to let go of that part of myself that believed such things could never happen to me. I realized in allowing myself to grieve for my friend without expectation, I had to do the same for my relationship with my husband. I had to go through it with eyes wide open, for I knew that if I blinded myself to any of it or missed any important lessons I'd simply attract conditions that would have me learn them later.

This experience has taught me something about living and dying. It is my job to live each day to the fullest – to express my feelings and myself truly, honestly and appropriately. Although I may question my inner voice because the things it tells me tend to be linearly incoherent, I realize that God is not linear. My still small voice is God speaking through me. It is God expressing through me. So It can express more completely as me. When I have the faith to trust that voice, each day has richness to it. I come away from each twenty-four hours with a sense of completeness. This, I believe, is the key to it all. In knowing how to live, I may perhaps also know how to die – to savor all of the new experiences that come and to transition with a sense of acceptance. The voice within is my connection to the Infinite; it is my Immortal self. As I align my consciousness with this all-knowing conduit, I relax into the truth of my being at all times during my life's passages.

## Life and Death
*David Alexander*

For most people death is not a subject that is easy to come to terms with. And on the other end of the scale, many people are living in fear and struggling because they are not living but rather just surviving another day. As I look around our society, I am overwhelmed by the amount of things we have created to extend life. Medicines, machines, diet programs, books that "you just gotta read" and all for what? If it was to enhance life's experience I would be okay with it. However, the more I think about it, the more it seems clear that there is a great fear in our society for death and we are trying everything in the book to avoid it. But no matter how hard or fast we run, we can't out run the inevitable. I have also taken amusement in noticing that some people who have lived the longest are not the heath nuts but rather the people who enjoyed life to the most. George Burns is an excellent example, well into his nineties he was hanging out with beautiful women and just having a good time! One of America's greatest runners died of a heart attack while running when he was only 43! What I have learned in life is that there is no finish line. There is no place to "get to" there is only the journey to be enjoyed. Death is not a thing to be feared, it is a natural process of life. It is simply a end of one expression of God and a beginning of another.

Learning to live is about learning to smell the roses of each day and to live from a place of deep gratitude for experiencing life once again. This is what Dr. Ernest Hohnes means when he writes about no one needing to prepare to meet God for they are meeting God in every moment of every day. Tell everyone you met how much you love them, you never know if it's your last chance or not.

## On Death and Dying
*"Happy" Shaw*

As death is one of my biggest fear issues, I wanted to pick a "safe" book to read about this subject. When I went to the library, *Death is of Vital Importance: On Life, Death, and Life After Death* by Elisabeth Kubler-Ross, M.D. seemed short enough so that I could get in and out of it quickly and get a paper written on it. What a surprise! Of course, it was exactly the book I needed to read and I was moved at how many of Dr. Kubler-Ross's young patients have no fear about dying at all. This seems to indicate all our fears about dying are picked up as we age.

Certainly during my growing up years, the death process was surrounded by fear-based memories dealing with adults' anger, conflict, shock and what I now know to be false beliefs about God and after-death judgment. Still I am not crazy about the idea of dying because I love it here on Earth and also because many people in my family have not died easily. In fact, most deaths in my family have been due to horrible diseases and long invalid years of suffering by both patient and the attending family members. Everything about death has always seemed like a bummer to me. However, through reading this book and my own good sense, I now know the death and dying experience does not have to be that way. In fact, I have had two experiences with "wonderful" funerals of two adult friends.

One was an older man who was a long time member of a church I used to attend whose funeral was the most upbeat and joyous I have ever attended, and another was for a dear woman who attended that same church and whom everyone loved. The feelings at the latter funeral were deeply touching but filled with a calmness that this wonderful woman's passing was somehow just as perfect as any other event or day God has made and will continue to make.

Another experience with my friend (I'll call Nancy) allowed

## got spirit?

me to witness someone's dying process close up. I had a ball of anger and guilt around it. I guess what shocked and angered me with Nancy's dying process was how little her own church and family members were prepared to do to help this young woman, who was dealing with tongue and throat cancer. Also my youngest daughter was diagnosed with juvenile diabetes at ten years old, right in the middle of Nancy's dying process. Thus I had a lot of stuff to go through dealing with that.

Frankly I felt overwhelmed with *even trying* to feed Nancy and her family or driving her to chemo the few times that I did. Along with my inability to get my daughter's diabetes under control, I felt exhausted and angry at the people in her church and other friends I felt should be helping her too. I was also diagnosed with Sojerns' syndrome during the same period and the Gulf War started. To say that this seemed like a time of plagues is putting it mildly.

Nancy had also found out her husband had been cheating on her and they had separated for a while before her illness progressed to the living in the hospital stage. Sometimes he seemed to be there for Nancy and sometimes not. Only a female relative in town seemed to be really there for Nancy throughout everything.

Once Nancy was hospitalized, I visited her there and we shared laughter and thoughts. We didn't know each other extremely well but were in a writing critique group together; however, I told her that she had taught me not to be afraid of dying. Then Nancy said that that must have been why she rallied after the first time the doctors had called her family, thinking she would die within days but she didn't. However, I did not really understand that after she rallied that she was actually going to die. So I really didn't face my deepest feelings about death at that time even though I innocently thought I had.

Some of my confusion stemmed from my having been told Nancy was going to receive a tube in her chest so that she could go home. Oddly enough, Nancy was afraid of having the tube put in. So I got my friend Suzie who had had one for years and years because of Crohn's disease to come into the hospital and talk to Nancy about it. I told Nancy that with the tube she would be able to go home and write. She seemed to think that was a fine idea too, as her dream was to write and sell her romance novels.

Later, I felt that I had been deceived by the family and possibly Nancy herself into believing she was recovering because the doctors were sending her home. I had no idea that she was being sent home to die. She had sat up in bed in the hospital, talked and laughed. I do not understand why they did not make this clear to me.

Once Nancy was at home, I also visited there. At first, she was still talking and asking about my youngest daughter's diabetic condition. Later, Nancy slipped into a coma, and my witnessing her slip into the deep rasping breathing of the dying process became too painful for me to watch, for all I could think of was my little daughter and her recent diagnosis of juvenile diabetes.

I felt guilty because I could not be there more for Nancy and that I really did not want to be there more. I felt I had all I could handle with my daughter's illness, but another friend of Nancy's and mine, a nurse, kept pushing me to go over to Nancy's house and to be even more a part of her dying process. *And I resented it.* All I could think of was that if I could not help my daughter get her diabetes under control she might die too, and the last thing I wanted to do was see Nancy actually die to reinforce my fears about my little daughter.

My nurse friend seemed to think I should put Nancy first, but I did not feel I could do that – nor did I want to. When I was a child, my own mother was always caring for someone in our huge extended family who was dying and I know I felt at those times I was not getting the attention I needed. Remembering those feelings from my own childhood, I decided I was not going to do that to my little daughter.

However, having been told by my nurse friend that Nancy considered me as her "best friend" made me feel even more conflicted and guilty for not being there for her. Now years later, after reading Dr. Kubler-Ross's book, I find my feelings back then were not all that unusual. Many people wind up with other crises in their lives while someone they know is dying and we often feel guilty because we cannot do everything for everybody. My friend Nancy was not at all a selfish person and even on her deathbed, she was concerned about my little daughter, as her daughter was only a year younger than mine. Nancy probably more than anyone else understood my need to take care of my child first.

Dr. Kubler-Ross's book dealt a lot with how to live one's life so that there is not a lot of what she calls "grief work" to be done as a person is dying. I have worked on a lot of my stuff. So I no longer carry a lot of anger against anyone anymore. Before my mother-in-law passed away, though we had never gotten on, I had written her a letter thanking her for the gift of her son and telling her what a wonderful husband and father he was. I am truly grateful for having done that.

From reading Kubler-Ross's book, I gained some new awareness about patients, even very young ones, being able to draw pictures of where the trouble was within their bodies. This seemed to be an extraordinarily useful bit of information which I am surprised other types of physicians are not using to patients' advantage. I have only had one physician, a chiropractic doctor, who actually asked me to draw a picture of my pain, and oddly enough, after having had tons of tests and x-rays, etc. scheduled by regular medical doctors before I went to him, he was the only one who correctly diagnosed what was wrong and was able to help me.

Also, I found in reading this book by the leading *expert* on death and dying that the pages were filled with the humaness of a unique individual from whom spiritual truths poured but who was also very realistic about having to keep working on herself. That made me feel I was, indeed, good enough and spiritual enough to be a minister or pastoral counselor. Because if Dr.

Kubler-Ross, *the expert on death and dying*, still had stuff which came up occasionally to work through, well, then I could too, and I still could be wonderful at working with others at the same time.

### PRAYER TREATMENT
*"Happy" Shaw*

***Purpose:***

This treatment is for the neutralization of childhood memories of relatives or friends' deaths and the fears associated with dying which resulted from these memories.

***Recognition:***

God is Everlasting. There is no end to God. God is Eternal. Everything that has been made has been created by God out of Its own Substance. Therefore, everything that has been made is Eternal. God is Life.

***Unification:***

I have been made by God. My life is eternal, just as the life of all things is eternal in Spirit. I am a precious part of God as is everyone else.

***Realization:***

I need not fear the end of my life as this human being, for I am a God-being. My spirit is without end, just as my <u>insert relative or friend's name's</u> spirit is without end. <u>Name</u> is also a part of God and their spirit is unending just as my spirit is unending.

God cannot destroy God. We humans will all live on in some new form. It is not necessary for me to know the nature of my continuing life, only to know that I will continue to live in God, of God, as part of God.

Death is a false belief. To God a death is only a new beginning, as nothing ever dies. It only takes a new form – Spirit ever unfolding upon Itself. As part of that Eternal Spirit, my Spirit lives, has always lived and will continue to live for all Eternity.

## *Thanksgiving:*

I give thanks that I need have no fears about death any longer, knowing that there is no death – only life – and that life is the Life of God and that Life is my life too.

## *Release:*

I release all fears of death or dying and go on about living. And so it is and so I let it be.

**got spirit?**

*My Notes On Death and Life*

## SECTION NINE

# *Ending Addictive Behaviors*

*"Awakening from our sense of separateness is what
we are called to do in all things."*
– Ram Dass

## Ending Addictive/Compulsive Behaviors
*David Alexander and Rebecca Allen*

To me, David (I'm still in my twenties but I think most people would agree) life is about finding your 'self'. It is a constant adventure of seeking for truth and sanity in a sometimes insane world. As we grow and learn, we construct our own concepts of reality. Each one of us constructs a life style that makes us comfortable and able to deal with life's "problems." There are a lot of things going on in the world that we must deal with. We worry about paying bills, finding work, being happy, getting along with people, being accepted, being worthy, guilt, stress, money, pollution, economy, global warming, and world peace! Wheew, this can be very overwhelming!

We each find ways of dealing with all of this and some people choose to avoid it. People try to escape and repress their problems by hiding behind habits. Habits like work, alcohol, drugs, sex, smoking, eating and many others all seem to take our problems away or make them bearable. For some people these addictions make the person feel whole, complete and acceptable. Whatever the reason it all seems to boil down to seeking something outside the self to complete the puzzle.

Most addictions can be traced back to an event or set of circumstances early in a person's life. Some seem to be caused by early childhood trauma, maybe sexual abuse, physical or verbal abuse in the early and critical stages of life. It is through these early developmental stages that we develop our sense of the world. Such traumatic events can not only affect our beliefs and thinking patterns but also our brain. Other factors that appear to cause or contribute to addictions are peer pressure, the desire to fit in, or the search for identity. I see this most commonly in teenagers and young adults. Often young people believe that smoking, drinking, having sex, etc, will help them in the quest to "fit in." It does not take long before personal choice turns into a mental and physical addiction.

Each of these so-called causes are really only on the surface. What I mean is that they appear to be the cause of our addictions. I do not mean to belittle these experiences or the addictions, indeed each is very real and needs to be treated seriously. I also believe that treatments for these surface level causes (or effects of something deeper) are very effective. Psychotherapy, hypnotherapy, psychological counseling, Twelve Step programs, rehabilitation (just to name a few) are all valuable and effective in the treatment of people with addictions regardless of the level of cause on which they focus. However, as I said, I believe that there is deeper root cause to each of these problems. Again, I state that it is a belief that someone or something outside of ourselves will make us whole or make our problems go away.

It has been my observation that when people engage in addictive behavior they feel that sense of completion, wholeness or cosmology but this feeling is temporary and only lasts as long as the behavior does.

It is a lack of cosmology that I believe to be the root cause of society's addictions and compulsive behavior. Having a healthy cosmology is to have a clear understanding of one's place in the Universe and our individual relationship to the Supreme Presence. When we have this, we understand that we do not need anything outside of ourselves to make us whole.

Jesus also taught us this lesson when he said, "Seek first the kingdom of God and all things will be added unto you." Not only did Jesus tell us that our lives would be fulfilled when we first sought the kingdom, he also told us where to find it! "Behold the Kingdom is within!" When we seek the Kingdom within, we are finding our personal cosmology, we are recognizing our unity with a Higher Power. Needs that are sought to be fulfilled in addictive behaviors are spiritual needs which can be truly fulfilled when we find that sense of cosmology. A cure to addictive behaviors begins with a willingness to pursue spiritual ideas and recognition of a Divine Power that is freedom, love and wholeness. Often it is not easy but it can be done.

What I, Rebecca, a mom of two nearly grown sons, know is that it is particularly hard for me to be critical of anyone who is addicted to anything. My life has been deeply touched by alcohol and I have been surrounded by alcoholics.

The dictionary definition of "addictive" is: "to devote or give oneself to, habitually or compulsively." The definition is as ambiguous as the general societal attitudes which surround addictions and compulsions. As a society, we are unable to decide if the cause of addictions is chemical, mental, emotional or hereditary. Even though we are unable to understand the cause, we tend, as a society, to label addicts as weak and lacking character. For my part, I believe additive behavior is just a way of seeking love and comfort. I believe addictive personalities are longing for peace and love. There seems to be a deep, sad part of the being which longs for soothing or nurturing and seeks something outside of itself for comfort, confidence and love. I think, no matter what the nature of addiction it is a call for love.

What I know is, alcohol alone is not necessarily bad. There are as many different kinds of drinkers as there are non-drinkers. Alcohol seems to magnify personality characteristics; if a person is sweet and good natured they will be more-so under the influence. If, however, a person is a nasty jerk, that particular part of their nature will be magnified when they are drunk.

Addictions, of all kinds, seem to serve to keep us numb and out of touch with our deep feelings and deep pains. I do not know, nor have I ever known, seen or heard of anyone who is happy, content and filled with self-confidence and self-love who is an addict.

I believe there are certain personalities which have a propensity for additions. For instance, many people may be addicted to cigarettes, alcohol, sugar and coffee. The same part of the brain is wired to urge one or all of these cravings – which indicates a strong physical connection. If the smoker tries to stop smoking, yet drinks alcohol, eats sugar or is a heavy coffee drinker, it is three times more difficult to stay off the cigarettes. It is easier to give up all of these things at one time than it is to give up just one. But, more than that, an alcoholic may give up liquor and be dismayed to find himself addicted to sex, gambling or some other addictive element.

It is said, and I believe it to be true, no matter what the trouble – love is the answer. I think, given the proper environment of unconditional love, understanding, support and self-esteem, everyone can be nurtured into sobriety.

Lacking those conditions, addicts have to white-knuckle themselves into abstinence. This is possible, but seldom ideal and the addict is always at risk of a relapse because the deep cause, a perceived separation from the God Source, is never addressed.

Given the definition mentioned earlier, "addictive" is: "to devote or give oneself to, habitually or compulsively," I think it is also possible to be addicted to seeking God. Just the knee-jerk reaction to that concept is a clear clue that the word, "addiction" carries a powerful, negative message. No matter, for now, seeking Spirit will be my addiction of choice because, I too am looking for peace, love and comfort. The difference is, I am turning to the power inside rather than an artificial substance.

## What I Believe To Be True About Addictive/Compulsive Behavior
*"Happy" Shaw*

Having been afflicted with addictive/compulsive behavior myself, I have completed a great deal of research and study in this area. Based on my own experience with OCD (obsessive compulsive disorder) and my research, I believe addictive/compulsive behavior is party biological and can be inherited genetically. In some cases, it can also be modeled behavior, such as entire families who smoke or drink to excess or even families who always eat lamb or turkey served a special way at holidays because "grandma did it that way."

Drinking to excess, smoking, obsessive thoughts, addictive sexual habits, obsessive hand washing, and all other addictive/compulsive behaviors are in fact ritualized behavior and fall within the realm of OCD. Some such as smoking and drinking also have special houses, like bars, in which the ritualized behavior is considered to be "normal." It is interesting that in mythology bars relate to the "watering hole" where all are equal and one goes to get information before entering the special world or underworld. Places where one eventually confronts one's own shadow self in the hero's journey myth. Also in mythology, a bar is seen as the "jumping off point" to enter the special or underworld, and interestingly enough, after becoming drunk at a bar, people often do jump off bridges, overpasses, and other high things, trying to end their lives or to leap into oblivion.

I believe most ritual habits aren't harmful, like eating certain foods on certain holidays in certain ways. However, harmful ritual behavior which results in emotional and mental illness may develop from a person's cell makeup being predisposed to addictive/compulsive behavior and a combination of other influences. In other words, though all the siblings in a family might be predisposed biologically to having OCD, it seems only the *very emotionally sensitive, extremely creative, or emotionally fragile persons* in the family actually develop the ritualizing behavior labeled as "sickness" or "not normal." I also believe emotional fragility can be caused by cell makeup but can be tremendously enhanced by physical and psychological abuse.

Three of the most interesting passages I found in my research were recorded centuries ago. The first was written in 1660 by Jeremy Taylor, a Cambridge-educated clergyman and writer, in a religious text titled *Doctor Dubitantium*. In this religious text, which is referred to in *The Boy Who Couldn't Stop Washing: The Experience & Treatment of Obsessive-Compulsive Disorder* by Dr. Judith L. Rapoport, M.D. (1989), it is said that Jeremy Taylor "gave case materials to show how religious scruples merge into obsession disorder, and then into madness: 'They repent when they have not sinn'd (sinned)... .' The church writers of Taylor's time felt the presence of the scruples actually *interfered* with an individual's religious development."(Page 237)

The second passage, written in 1522-23, by Ignatius Loyola also cited in the Rapoport book, reads "After I have trodden upon a cross formed by two straws, or after I have thought, said or done some other thing, there comes to me from 'without' a thought that I have sinned, and on the other hand it seems to me that I have not sinned; nevertheless I feel some uneasiness on the subject, inasmuch as I doubt yet do not doubt." (Page 236)

And the third passage, again cited in the Rapoport book, from 1730, "Saint Alphonsus Liguori descried scrupulosity as a groundless fear of sinning that rises from 'erroneous ideas.'" (Page 236)

These enlightened viewpoints, having been written in 1660, 1522-23, and 1730, really astounded me because I had always felt I was "religiously damaged." Also I had always believed if had I not been convinced as a young child through the constant repetition of hearing the "fire and brimstone" teachings of sin and punishment, I perhaps would not have developed OCD at all or to the extent to which I did. Also, I feel certain religious teaching about a fearful and judgmental God are the root cause of many people's emotional and mental problems involving addictive/compulsive behavior.

When I observed an AA meeting as part of a class assignment, I heard two people share what negative experiences they had had as children – and even as adults – with religion. They described how they had to learn from AA, of all places, that God was a loving, supportive power to help them stop drinking, and they also described how they still had problems with religious people and church.

I am not suggesting all compulsive/addictive behavior should be overlooked. I believe ritual sexual abuse, which causes harm to others, and drunken driving are extremely dangerous to other people as well as the person exhibiting the behavior.

However, as for the less dangerous (to others) compulsive/addictive behaviors, I believe a spiritual recovery program could be a great supplement to programs like AA or other groups. Science of Mind and my new belief in a totally loving God is the only thing, which has, even come close to healing my OCD. What some traditionally trained health professionals don't seem to realize is once a person stops smoking, drinking, abusing, etc. through other means (AA, will power, or whatever) the person is not really healed inside. They have simply stopped exhibiting an outside problem behavior. It doesn't mean the inside thought of not being good enough has been cleaned up. In fact, one can give up drinking and substitute overeating or smoking instead, still trying to fill up the hole in the soul.

It is interesting that ritual behavior has some of the repetitive aspects of grooming in animals. By grooming each other, which is really an act of acceptance into the tribe, the animal feels he is a part and belongs. And oddly enough, many of the people who feel separated from God, themselves and others, will take up ritualistic behaviors such as hand washing, pulling out hair, and excessive washing of their environment, in an attempt to do for themselves what was not done by their human tribe – making them feel accepted and loved unconditionally.

Addictive/compulsive people are trying to fill up a hole inside of them – a hole where God should be. However, they believe they aren't worthy of God's attention, and in some cases having been told as much by authority figures, they feel totally separated from God – which we know in metaphysical religious and psychological terms means they feel separated from their true self or higher self – truly their God self.

In my opinion, until someone starts teaching the spiritual recovery program, compulsive/addictive behavior may stop, but it will simply go underground. The person won't be completely healed until they, as Thomas Moore says, "are given back to themselves" and they come to know who they really are and that they are not the "bad" person they thought they were and they understand and truly know they are accepted by God.

I don't really consider my addictive/compulsive behavior as deviant any longer and know it is simply my soul's outward manifestation of trying to get the attention it needs. However, I do not want to be around people who are smoking and I don't allow people to smoke in my house. I also do not like to be around people who are out of control due to excessive drinking. I know from experience how dangerous both these behaviors can be to others. A friend died from her husband's second hand smoke and too many women are raped by drunken men.

Some people simply have such a horrible time constantly listening to the condemning voices in their head that tell them they are bad or a sinner or whatever that they believe the only way they can survive is to blot it all out. The ritual habit is a way to take the focus off the underlying problem of not feeling good about one's self.

Unfortunately, the chosen ritualistic behavior can turn out to be worse than the original problem. For instance, I knew a woman who became an alcoholic in order to deal with her agoraphobia.

Had she been able to learn how to deal with the first ritual behavior – agoraphobia, avoiding places to avoid feeling fear – she then wouldn't have had the much more serious alcohol problem. I think this is a classic example of not dealing with cause and the problems just keep multiplying, trading one for another, or building one on top of another. People who smoke often drink. People who smoke and drink <u>sometimes</u> eat too much or abuse children or other adults. On and on and on.

If I have a position at all on the subject of addictive/compulsive behavior, I would say it is natural rituals gone awry. If the child had been honored, showered with love and gifts honoring its presence and blessed as a manifestation of God's love, it would never have splintered off from is true self and sought solace outside itself in compulsive/addictive behaviors.

As for creating parents and religious institutions that understand how to recognize God in each other, America has failed miserably. It is truly sad religions based on fear are still packing them in today. Addictive/compulsive behaviors are also tremendously on the rise in our society and are affecting younger and younger children.

I honestly believe metaphysical religious studies saved my life and can truly say that except for the grace of God, I would have ended my life in a bottle or on "medically prescribed drugs" or by driving over a cliff because the pain of my addictive/compulsive behavior had become more than I could bear. All I could think of back then was killing myself. And all I can think of today is making my life even more wonderful.

As a spiritual counselor, I would like to be a beacon of light to those who have experienced OCD and feel they are separated from God.

## PRAYER TREATMENT
*Jeannie Bullard*

### *Recognition:*

There is one Universal Mind, one Principle, one Substance, one Source, one Relationship. Spirit is infinite and eternal Divine Givingness and Unconditional Love. Spirit is life and life is the consciousness of love and companionship.

### *Unification:*

I am a creation of Spirit made from Universal-Substance as a unique spiritual expression. Spirit made me out of Itself by direct contemplation. I move and live and have my being as a thought held in Divine Mind. <u>Insert Name</u> is also called into being by special invitation of the One Mind.

Directly evolved from God-Stuff, he/she is a channel for Divine Love and Companionship. He/She is a living reflection of the Spiritual Relationship.

### *Realization:*

<u>Name</u> cannot be alone. Divine Love and Companionship accompanies him/her always. This personal relationship with the Creator of all things is intimate, close and supportive. All the power there is waits to serve him/her, waits upon his/her direction. This power is incapable of abandonment and is forever present in its fullness in each moment of his/her life. He/She cannot be separated from Spiritual Love. He/She is embraced by the Divine Givingness of the One. Love resides at the center of his/her being. This center of Love which is <u>Name,</u> reaches out into the Universe attracting all that is his/hers by Divine Right. The love <u>Name</u> is seeking is also seeking him/her. It is present now, this moment and cannot be kept from him/her. The entire Cosmos aligns behind his/her desire to manifest unconditional love and support. <u>Name</u> accepts this new realization and his/her consciousness expands to accept all there is into his/her life. He/She is lifted up and empowered by this eternal relationship with

his/her Divine Source. *Name* and God are inseparable. He/She lives in fulfilling partnership with the Creator of All. Infinite Love is now his/her ever present reality. He/She begins right where he/she is to give of himself/herself. Gifting love to all in his/her life, opening his/her heart with compassion. Through his/her own channeling of unconditional love, *Name* receives, returning tenfold, gifts in kind – love, compassion, respect and support. The law of attraction never fails, love rushes in to fill his/her experience.

### *Thanksgiving:*

I am thankful for the ever present companionship of the Divine in *Name's* life and for his/her opportunity to open to, and experience the limitless influx of Divine Love.

### *Release:*

I release my word into the creative substance of Law, knowing that it is already accomplished. I allow it to be and so it is.

## SECTION TEN

## *Forgiveness*

"Sometimes I go about pitying myself
While I am carried by
The wind
Across the sky."

– Native American Chippewa Song

## Forgiveness of the Past Releases the Present
*"Happy" Shaw*

In all relationships, forgiveness connects people on a heart level by discarding all past patterns of relating. If we learn to forgive and let the past go, the Creative Principle will operate toward our Good and no longer operate on what has gone before. And we will no longer keep repeating old relationship patterns within our own consciousness. I say "our own consciousness" because forgiveness relates to putting ourselves back in alignment with Spirit – not the other person. Forgiveness is always about what we held against the other person – even if what we held against them was deemed "wrong" in terms of the way the world or society sees things.

The fact is that God or Spirit does not see as we see. Spirit only sees perfection as God created it. If it is hard to see "perfection" in someone who has abused us or hurt us in some way, what we are actually holding on to is the fact that it is hard for us to see it in ourselves.

For instance, if we have experienced abuse in any form, we may subconsciously think we are a bad person or must have deserved the pain we experienced. Since we are holding the hurt to ourselves like a dragon's treasure, we often fill ourselves with fire. This angry fire usually turns against us and burns us. It does nothing to the person who hurt us. By holding onto our hurts so and refusing to forgive, we think it hurts those who hurt us – but it does not. It only hurts us.

This is what is meant in the Bible when it talks of vengeance belonging to the Lord. If we try to judge in place of Divine Judgment, then we only wind up hurting ourselves.

This is not to say that what another person may have done to us or others is acceptable behavior. However, forgiveness comes in realizing that what they did is not who they are as Spirit sees them. Our task in our own healing is to see our Spiritual selves as never damaged and to see others, whoever they are, in the same light. If we can not afford them the same light, then we have no light to shine from ourselves.

In forgiveness, everything and everyone is striped down from surface layers to the Divine Source. We experience each feeling in the present moment as Perfect, each thought, word and deed as Perfect in Spirit even though what we "see" with our outer directed senses may look much less than "right" or "perfection in action." Letting go of the past in forgiveness and looking beyond current worldly appearances of "right" or "wrong" and clearing away any judgments about a person – we are or have been in relationship with – is very freeing.

However, we must be truly present in the moment and know that he/she and ourselves are expressions of Spirit and that expression is Perfect – no matter what kind of surface layer may be manifesting as a perceived "problem" by the other person or our worldly self. Then we can see as God sees. Our conflicted nature will fall away and we can experience peace whether the other person chooses to or not.

Yet if the other person is open to changing their thinking, and thus their life, we can help them see that going to a deeper level of letting go of the past through forgiveness and just living in the present can enhance their experience of Life and Love in all their relationships.

However, especially with situations of abuse, rape or molestation, the other person may often have retreated into their intellect to insulate themselves from the pain and also from a world that they now feel they can no longer trust. By being quiet and just listening and being with the other person, we can experience the moment whether the other person is truly present in the moment or not. They may be reliving their past. However, by our really connecting on a Spiritual level with them, knowing who they really are, and our setting up an atmosphere of love where they feel safe, the other person may feel more comfortable to express and truly feel more of the negative emotions that they may, up until this time, have been suppressing.

Once they have talked out what they perceive as their problem, then we can calmly and quietly start to ask questions, trying to focus the person on the present moment and establishing the fact that no matter what has happened in the past, that we are now in control of our reactions to it within the only real moment, which is the present.

We can then bring up the question of whether they wish to continue to give power to whatever is bothering them and keeping them from expressing happiness and joy within themselves today.

Once we have established that there is a way out of living in one's head all the time and in the past, we can teach the other person about awareness of living in the present moment by letting the past go in forgiveness.

### PRAYER TREATMENT
*"Happy" Shaw*

**Purpose:**
This treatment is for clarity and loving acceptance of childhood memories.

**Recognition:**
God is everything and everything is good, as it is made of God. There cannot be anything made and nothing can occur that is not Good, for all is God and all is Good.

**Unification:**
I am part of God's creation, and as such, everything about me is also Good. I am a good person, a good human being, expressing as God in human form, but my true nature is Spirit – that of the Spirit of God. I am not all of God, but God fills and surrounds all of me.

***Realization:***

Nothing that happened to me as a child can have power over me, as God is All, and therefore, all power is God's. I realize that these childhood incidents and memories are as neutral as Spirit. I no longer wish to act out of false beliefs caused by unclear thinking. My thinking is now clear. I am filled with clarity that my experiences are just that – my experiences – and I can make of them what I wish. Going back to Spiritual Truth, I wish to make them return to the nothingness from which they came. They no longer have any effect over any part of my being, body, mind or spirit. My Spirit is free, my body is free, and my mind is free of any negative influence that I may have allowed to occur through unclear thinking about my childhood memories. God is making everything new. I am washed clean, my mind is clear, my thoughts are focused, and my body is healed. I lovingly accept my childhood memories as just that – only memories – and not Spiritual Truth. The only Spiritual Truth is that All is Good, for All is God.

***Thanksgiving:***

I give thanks for the clarity of thinking that is now mine, and for the release of any false beliefs that I have carried with me into my present life. I joyfully receive these blessings of Truth.

***Release:***

And so I reflect these Truths in my present life and let them be.

## got spirit?

*My Notes About Forgiveness In My Life*

# SECTION ELEVEN

# *Oneness*

*"You are in me and I am in the Father."*
– Jesus, *New Testament*

## One With God
*Rebecca Allen*

What does it mean to be one with God? I have only a vague clue. Giving this point some thought, I discover the overwhelming idea of being one with God is so awesome that I can only allow one little speck of possibility of Oneness to seep into my awareness, one little speck at time.

To understand Oneness is a learning process. We have been taught separation and fear for so long, it is deeply ingrained in our minds. A flash of revelation would be wonderful, but for most of us, it is a steady chipping away at the old belief system, minute by minute, day by day. I can intellectually grasp the concept that I am One with all that is, but to get it deep down is harder to do. I just have to keep chipping away at all of the old stuff, buffing and polishing away at the scratches and imperfections until the underlying beauty of the Truth shines through.

When I know I am One, then all illusions which cause fear will disappear – fear has no place in God. All limits will disappear because God's Universe is limitless. It is always easier to see the truth about others. As I see the truth about others, it will become easier to see the truth about myself.

When I know I am One, then I will demonstrate all the attributes of God. I will be unconditional love; I will be peace; I will be joy; I will be harmony, and I will be wisdom. I will know who I am and I will know the truth of all.

### PRAYER TREATMENT
*Rebecca Allen*

***Purpose:***
To deny the Race Thought which believes that with age the body and mind deteriorate.

***Recognition:***
There is one Mind, that One Mind is all there is. The One

Mind is ageless, changeless, timeless and infinite. The One Mind activates, integrates, surrounds and permeates all that is. Nothing is excluded, nothing is forgotten and nothing is lost.

### *Unification:*

Because One Mind is All, I know my being, my body and my mind are integrated, surrounded and permeated with the energy, power and force that we call God. Nothing about my mind, body or spirit is ever excluded, forgotten or lost because God surrounds, sustains and directs my every thought, action and deed.

### *Realization:*

I know, because I am one with the Divine Power, my every thought, action and deed is made fresh, clear and bright with the vigor of God's infinite energy. As God's strength and power flows through me, I am forever renewed, vitalized and energized with ageless, changeless Divine Energy. As an expression of God in action, my body, mind and spirit are constantly nourished and replenished. I know all thoughts of aging, decline and deterioration are shadows of a false belief. In God's Truth, my mind is forever bright and sharp, my skin is forever smooth, soft and supple, my vision is forever clear and accurate. As God in action, my body is agile, straight and powerful. I dance to a Universal Song.

### *Thanksgiving:*

I accept this truth for myself. I give thanks that as God in action, I am forever active, vigorous, alert and joyful. I accept and adore the ageless, changeless God Expression that I am.

### *Release:*

I now speak these words into Law. I know the truth of my words, with certainty, joy and gratitude, I let them be so and so it is.

## What It Means to be One
*Jeannie Bullard*

I am an avenue and channel of God expressing in creative form. God is Infinite Intelligence. I am part of that Self-knowing intelligence. There is no separation, nothing withheld for I Am what I desire. I do not *ask* in prayer or treatment. I *acknowledge* the Truth. There is no need to seek, for *I AM* what I am seeking. I am looking for what I am looking with. Separation is a manmade illusion. I turn from this to my inner intuitive knowing. When I live from the outside in, I give credence to the illusion of separation. I begin now to live from the inside out and all illusion works towards my good. Things are not my goal, they are added unto me when I rest in the center of the *ONE*. I know my inheritance. The veil is pierced and all is illumined as the body of God, one substance, one mind, one love, one life, One! I enter the sanctuary of a deeper reality. There is nothing to give, do, take or be. *I AM*.

The Allness of God is embodied within me, the infinite resides here. There is one Mind in the Universe. When a hologram is cut into many smaller pieces, even the smallest piece – when light is allowed to shine through it – projects the whole image. This powerful example reminds me that my task is to clear my mind, allowing the Light and Love of the One to flow in completeness and wholeness to the world. Consciously and directly, I align my perspective with the Light. As a part of Spirit, I am able to project the entirety of It. I carry within myself the Universe – the infinity of the All. I live, move and have my being immersed in the Spirit of Living Intelligence which expresses through me.

*Love, Joy, Peace, and Wisdom.*
*I am inseparably one with God.*

## Shades of Oneness
*"Happy" Shaw*

I believe that to be One, we as professed believers of Truth need to practice what we preach. If someone looks or acts a little odd to us, or is dressed somewhat differently, we need to be open to receive whatever lesson or gift that knowing or being in contact with that person will provide. If we shut down and refuse to truly *see* the person, or even a place or a thing with God's eyes, and we see them *as less than*, we not only deny the very Truth that we profess to know, but we also deny ourselves an opportunity to see a different facet of God, to learn something more about God's creative nature, and to ultimately learn more about ourselves.

Relationships are often hard for me. I have a hard time, usually at first, trusting other people. I am getting to the point though, of not letting myself get emotionally involved in how others react. This may be the door that is opening for me into learning what it means to be One. By that I mean being One within myself, and feeling I don't need others to make me feel whole, then I may soon start attracting people who also are whole within themselves and go on to establish the type of fulfilling relationships I have always wanted. I don't mean to say that I don't want to be dependent on others for anything, as I believe "being One" means there are things or gifts others can bring to a relationship which should be welcomed and appreciated. However, I have given up looking for Oneness outside of myself – commonly known as *codependency*.

Right now, I am not a bud yet, nor a flower, but a seed sprouting underground. Leaving codependency behind and making room to learn about Oneness can be lonely. I have spent many years alone with myself and my writing. I am trying to be okay with that, letting my sprout of Oneness have some silence to grow in. Perhaps this has been the true gift in starting a business, an outgrowth of my writing. It gave me something else to focus on, reducing the time I spent obsessing on past "stuff," creating some order within the monkey mind that had controlled me for so long.

Now I am seeing God in most things. I especially like using the blessing secretly in my own mind that John the Baptist used with Jesus, blessing him as God's precious child, in whom the Divine Presence is well pleased. I like blessing animals and plants that way, and I am moving into seeing all people in this manner, even those that I don't "like" and don't want to spend social time with because they harm others. It is good to be able to bless them, and also release them and not have to have them creating chaos in my life.

This is not denying the Oneness of All. It is only living a life of choice, allowing myself to chose what and who I have in my life. Even illusions that the world perceives as "disasters" of events and destructive human beings can be blessed and released and not concentrated upon. It is not to say I am denying what is happening in the physical world, and that bad news is not part of the Oneness. It is just that I feel happier and more centered if I don't lay myself down as a doormat for bad news or destructive human beings to enter my life. I cannot accept that being upset all the time does anything for helping one to *see* Oneness.

Before Joseph Campbell died, he said two things about the positive and negative sides of Oneness. The first was "follow your bliss," meaning follow the positive things in your life, those that enhance it. The second was "God is horrific," and he laughed saying it, indicating there are a lot of things in life which we view as unpleasant or bad and that things change sometimes drastically and in ways we think we don't want, but it is all just part of being alive.

In the natural environment, we must learn which plants to take home and beautify our houses and which plants are poison ivy or the like. To believe we can change something's nature simply because we want to or believe it should be different than it is can lead to sickness within ourselves and our "houses" – our Spiritual Consciousness. This is how codependency works. Since we have the mistaken belief people do not have a right to make their own choices, we try to take care of them and set them "right." Often leading to sickness within ourselves. The whole thing goes awry in the beginning because we don't see "We are all One" in the first place. Just as poisonous plants have their place and purpose, poisonous people have their place in the Oneness.

We need to appreciate them where they are and for what they are and their purpose, even if God Spirit is the only One who knows what that purpose is. But it does not mean that those "negative" aspects of the Oneness are to be removed from their place, against their will, and held to our breasts. I think the most important thing we could possibly learn is that no one needs to be healed at all. And if they suddenly seem to be healed, our little illusion of our separate body/mind/ego/personality isn't the ONE doing the healing.

Though there are times I no longer judge people and know we are all One, I am also now into trying to stay at a place where I am not stressed out all the time. Or angry. Or upset. I like feeling happy, and now that I know what feeling happy really feels like I want more of that feeling. I want to look past the horrific stuff to Oneness. Being One within myself first, and perhaps, after I become practiced at *Being Who I am* and what I want to do with the knowledge of *Who I am*, I will see more clearly what it is that I want to do.

When I can go back out into the world and not see the "horrific" any more than Jesus saw it in a Spiritual sense, then I will truly know what it means to be One with the Father while living *in* the world and at the same time not being *of* the world.

## PRAYER TREATMENT
*"Happy" Shaw*

**Purpose:**

To see the Presence of God in all people and all religions.

**Recognition:**

There is only one God, creator and self-existent Cause of All that is.

**Unification:**

I, called in this life by my human name, am created by God out of Itself. I am a divine child of God put on this earth at this time for the purpose of being in God as a part of God. Like myself, all other people are also created by God out of Itself and fulfill a unique purpose unto themselves as one with God.

**Realization:**

I realize that each person created by God has free will, and therefore, can chose freely what they wish to believe about God. Their truth is their truth and is just as valuable to them as my truth is to me. Their idea or understanding of God is perfect for them in this life as mine is for me. I may not like or accept for myself some of the facets of their chosen religion, but I accept their right to choose for themselves to worship in any manner which feels helpful to them. God is wiser than I can ever be because I only share a part of God's mind. As God has a purpose for me, I am sure God has a purpose for each individual and a purpose for that person's religious faith.

**Thanksgiving:**

I give thanks that I can accept others of different faiths as they are and not have to "save" them or bring them to thinking and accepting my view of God or the Universe. I give thanks, knowing all people are as precious to God as I am.

**Release:**

I release these words and so it is and so I let it be.

# SECTION TWELVE

## Trust

"May I be filled with loving-kindness. May I be well.
May I be peaceful and at ease. May I be happy."
– From a Buddhist Meditation

## Trust
*Tammy L. Young*

In thinking about Trust, we may come to realize we have reconnected with some of the teachings of our youth. There are many ways in which the Bible and other Sacred Writings encourage us to Trust in a Divine Intelligence.

- "God will never put upon you more than you can withstand."

For a long period of time, this statement was offensive to me for many reasons. Now, I feel that there should be an *if* in that statement. *If* I trust in the Divine Power of the Universe to guide me, protect me, and teach me, then I see my experiences in such a way that I can handle anything.

- "The Lord will keep in perfect peace all those who trust in Him." My grandmother gave me a little knic-knac with this quotation. It has come to mean a lot to me, for I find it to be absolute. By trusting that Spirit within me, I know that everything is in perfect order and I do not need to worry, fret, or fear. I am in perfect peace.

I also see that when I am in a place of complete trust, I experience greater love. I experience love in every moment. When I trust that Spirit goes before me on the roadway and clears a safe path for my travel, I do not need to be angered by anyone else's behavior. I am free to experience love in that moment because I know that I am safe and instead of cursing the other driver, I can bless him and say a prayer for his safety and those traveling near him.

It is the same in every situation. I do not need to experience a negative interaction with people because I know Spirit put me there to experience something different.

## PRAYER TREATMENT
*Tammy L. Young*

### Recognition:

There is one Power and Presence in the Universe. That Power and that Presence is one of Love and Peace. This awesome Power is all-knowing, wise beyond words. It is Clarity and Acceptance. This Presence is the presence of Wholeness and Harmony. This Power and Presence is God. God is. God is all there is.

### Unification:

I am a spiritual being. I live and move and have my being in the Presence of God. I am a part of God and God is all of me. My life is God's life. I am one with God and one with all that God is. I am Love and Peace. I am all-knowing and wise beyond words. I am Clarity and Acceptance. I am Wholeness and Harmony. This is the truth of my being.

### Realization:

I know that every moment of my life has been a process of unfoldment as a spiritual being. I know that every situation, every condition, every perceived hardship, and every moment of joy has been an expression of wholeness and harmony. There is absolute clarity in my mind now – I see clearly the love and the harmony of my life. I now accept every moment of my life as unfolding perfection. My every memory is recalled with awareness and fullness of Love and Peace. I now release any and all animosities or resentments that may have been held in subconscious mind, knowing that the truth of my being and the truth of my life is perfect God, perfect life, perfect me.

### Thanksgiving:

It is with great joy that I know this truth of my being and of my life's experiences. I give thanks for this awareness, for every life experience, and for the continuing process of unfoldment ever present in my life.

**Release:**

I release these words now into the Law of Cause and Effect, knowing that as I have spoken them, they have already been manifest. And so it is, and so I let it be.

## TRUST
*Barbara Fox*

Trust is one of those things I usually examined in depth when a confidence was shared or during the life-threatening scenes in the movies. Bringing it to a more personal level of consciousness opens up a whole new avenue of contemplation and causes me to go a little deeper, to really ask myself the rather difficult question: "How do I demonstrate trust?"

I find I alternate between being too trusting and mistrusting. Trust is an area for me where balance is occasionally achieved, but usually not as much as I would like. Three ways in which it is possible for me to demonstrate trust are: going with the flow, faking it till I make it, and doing the simple mundane things when I do not know what to do next.

Going with the flow signifies a trust in the overall plan of Spirit, even though my ego may feel bewildered at the current circumstances. When things happen, as in the case of an impending change in my job situation, I practice trust in Spirit to provide me with that which is for my highest and best good by simply going with the flow of the situation. Interactions with others may signal to me that an emergency is forthcoming, but I try to regard each occurrence as part of a whole that may not be immediately evident to me now. I take a detached observer's approach in each happening along the way, trying not to react or predict (I tend to catastrophize) and simply say to myself, "Oh, isn't that interesting," instead of "I am doomed!" which is what I often said in the past. In observing and acknowledging that what I am seeing is a part of a whole I cannot perceive yet, I am trusting that Spirit is taking me somewhere always better then where I currently am, even though I cannot see it yet.

Faking it till I make it implies a trust that Spirit wants me to have my heart's desire. As a recovering compulsive overeater, I have had a rather warped, perversely self-centered image of myself. I pictured myself as less than others at some times and supremely better at others. As I grow in recovery, I come to realize that I am a unique child of God, just as special as his many other children are. This means that I am entitled to the gifts of Spirit just as my brothers and sisters are. Often though, it is the plight of the addict to have a short memory, and I forget and revert to feeling like a disenfranchised stepchild. It is during these times that "faking it till I make it" comes in very handy. By pretending to believe what I have ostensibly forgotten, I trust that my attitude will eventually realign with Spirit and I will once again be calmly recognizing my birthright.

The third way I practice trust is through doing the mundane things when I do not know what the big picture is saying. This is currently the theme for my days. There has been so much talk of ending my current work arrangement that panic seems to want to settle in at every turn. Should I look for another job? What do I want to do? Should I approach them before they approach me? Should I quit on principle? Should I bite the bullet and stay with an eight-hour workday even though right now it feels like death? All these questions feel unanswerable right now. My only recourse, now that using food and self-destructive behaviors to obliterate the discomfort of not knowing are no longer available, is to look around me and do the mundane things. I am finding the real intrinsic benefits in the modified saying, "When the going gets tough, the tough do dishes." Now, when I feel I am at a crossroads and filled with fear about the future, I direct my attention elsewhere. What needs to be done around the house? Are the animals fed? Do the plants need water? Have I paid the bills? Did I return the neighbor's garden hose? Is the laundry folded and put away? This way, I am effective in my immediate environment, my house looks neater, (which in turn contributes to my serenity) and I allow Spirit to do what Spirit does, while I do what I know I can do. This represents a trust that God is always operating for my highest and best good even when I cannot see it. It is through these three methods: going with the flow, faking it till I make it and doing the mundane things before me that I demonstrate trust in the goodness of my Higher Power, whom I call God or Spirit. I am grateful to have learned these behaviors. They have proven themselves practical, effective and constructive.

## Faith is Trust
*Jeannie Bullard*

Faith is *trust*, either in things seen or unseen. Its origins are from an innate, inner knowing, an expectation of order, being and outcome. Trust in Spirit has always been a companion of man to help apply safety and comfort to those things he cannot understand or control. As an original companion, faith, or trust, is of man and therefore, is man. Trust is a gift from our original source. A tool for re-connection. A safety line tethered to the Universal. Man has freedom to impress his own unique personality upon this Trust.

Trust constitutes our foundation of beliefs in the originating visible and invisible causation. Trust shapes our receptivity and perspective of Truth. It reveals our inner expectations and convictions, our perceptions of life. Trust forms through experience and the knowledge of outcomes, sure and anticipated. We shape our trust, or faith, through our own trial and error as well as by the acceptance of race consciousness. So, the beliefs that define our world are borrowed or personally proven or accepted. They are built upon the law of probabilities, averages and confident expectations, observation, experience and sometimes vestiges of lives already lived. Trust becomes an essence, a quality of mind as unique as the individual. Our trust and expectancy is an intimate, personal power. It consists of assurance and conviction. Trust is based on the character of our ideas planted in the mind by expectant attention. Carefully cultivated mental habits comprise our basic beliefs.

Trust functions to mold our reality. It is the foundation upon which we build, our reflecting mirror. It directs our manifestations and demonstrates our mental approach to reality. Trust, or faith, is the emotional fire, the inspirational source that partners with will and desire to manifest our thoughts. Trust is an important ingredient needed to arouse the dormant, latent or static. It initiates dynamic action through its emotional nature. It gives rise to enthusiasm and positive faith. It is the emotional essence of our foundational thought life. It stimulates and enlivens the intellect. Without the ingredient of trust, it would be almost impossible to manifest a desired outcome. A lack of faith, or trust, paralyzes manifestation. Negative faith, or lack of trust, does not stimulate enthusiasm and inhibits and deadens. Trust is confident expectation. It is our inspirational vision.

### PRAYER TREATMENT
*Happy Shaw*

**Purpose:**

To strengthen trust in God in all areas of my life.

**Recognition:**

God is Everything and manifests through everything.

**Unification:**

I am part of God and God manifests through me in every area of my life.

**Realization:**

There is no fear in God, and so there can be no fear within me concerning any area of my life. There is no need for concern because God is All and All is Good. Nothing but Good can come to me in any area of my life, for all I put into and out from any area of my life is Good. I am Good because God is Good and I am part of God. Therefore, my life is Good. My trust comes from knowing Who I am and Who lives through me as me.

**Thanksgiving:**

I am so thankful for every knowing of Truth that I own in my heart. I am so thankful that I have chosen the path to recognize and experience the Presence as working through and around me for Good.

**Release:**

I let go of any concerns about trusting in God and know that God is my rock and my salvation. And so it is and so I let it be.

**got spirit?**

*My Notes About Trust in My Life*

# SECTION THIRTEEN

## Healing

*"Be ye transformed by the renewing of your mind…"*
– New Testament, Romans 12:2

## Thoughts About Healing
### Barbara *Fox*

In my studies of metaphysics, I have come to understand that health is a natural state of being for all. Because God is all and it is the nature of God to be perfect, vibrant and whole, so it is the nature of us to be so as well. In my early studies, though, I had to wonder about such a so-called Universal Law with all the evidence of illness around me. Someone always seems to be "catching the crud," suffering from allergies, battling a diabetes-related condition, or withdrawing from addiction to cigarettes. During the two years of my in depth Spiritual study, a friend of mine was diagnosed with MS. The whole barrage of seemingly contradictory information caused me to wonder, *If perfect health is such a natural state, why then, are all my friends feeling so lousy?* For that matter, *Why was I feeling so at the mercy of my eating disorder? And what about the emotional instability?* I lamented. *What about the depression, the headaches, the frustration, and the inability to get off the couch and exercise?* For all the good work I had done, my life often seemed a poor reflection.

In my earliest days in recovery, I heard an audio taped copy of *You Can Heal Your Life* by Louise Hay. Unsure of how recovery would manifest in my life, her writing somehow served to lay a framework for my walk through the Twelve Steps. She talked of a standard of good health, and it was my first notion that health was a standard condition we all were eligible to obtain. At 220 lbs., I had given little thought to such an abstract concept as "vibrant health."

With Hay's words guiding me, I began working the program of Overeaters Anonymous. Not surprisingly, I experienced immediate results. My weight dropped, I released numerous old patterns and made peace with many issues which had inhibited my growth on physical, emotional and spiritual levels.

From this experience, I came to flirt with the idea of "having it all." For me, this meant a healthy body, freedom from addiction, physical flexibility, clarity of mind, and creative self-expression. (As I write this, I smile at its similarity to Louise Hay's definition.) From within, I began to hear the still small voice that had a pattern of wellness tailor-made for me. The definition came from inside, presumably from Spirit, directing me, acting as me, guiding me to my highest form of self-expression. It is through this that the concept of healing myself into health began to gel in my own consciousness.

Rediscovering health has come to mean the release of all false beliefs, outmoded behavioral patterns, and incorrect notions of God in order to allow the natural state of perfection to express. This has not been an overnight process for me. Although the revelation may have struck me like a lightning bolt, my willingness to release that which no longer serves me has been far more gradual.

My constant struggle with the human tendency to hold onto the familiar has kept me from shining "too brightly, too quickly." I alternately take comfort in and lament this aspect of my little self. As I heal, I see myself gradually relinquishing the need to be right, lack of trust in God, irrational fear, and a host of other traits I have misused. It is humbling to know that even though I may intellectually come to know these things, that until I come to know them in my heart, I will continue to struggle with them.

Now, when I look at the dilemmas of my friends, I am able to behold them with a compassionate heart, for their struggles are my struggles. My friend with MS, the people quitting smoking, battling allergies, diabetes-related conditions, or catching the crud, are manifesting their unresolved issues for them to see more clearly. Louise Hay has gone so far as to claim a standard mental causation for every condition in her little book *Heal Your Body*. Although I feel that such detail is not necessary here, suffice it to say, that like my friends, I experience my depression, frustration, bodily aches and pains and eating disorder because I am face-to-face with a belief or beliefs that no longer *got spirit?*

serve me. The conflict is evident in the condition itself. By letting go and courageously moving toward that which inwardly calls, we move toward the light of Spirit, and cannot help but heal into our birthright. As a matter of absolute certainty, healing ourselves into health is the natural result.

## Healing and Health
*Dave Schultz*

My concept of personal health has expanded through my Spiritual studies, but before this time of study, I thought of personal health in terms of only physical health. I now regard personal health as having several aspects – physical emotional, mental, financial, and spiritual. There may be more aspects as well. When I think of a perfectly healthy individual, I now consider all of those aspects. The same conditions must exist in a person if he/she is to enjoy perfect health in any one of those aspects.

Personal health is not a goal; it is a consciousness and a way of being. If I perceive personal health as a goal, that implies that it is something I don't already have. In that case, I am operating on a belief of separation from personal health. So, I choose to approach the concept of personal health as something that is already mine, one of continuing consciousness. I think of all the aspects of my life as playing out perfectly, and I visualize freely flowing supplies of certain qualities coming into and through my life, expressing as perfect health. Qualities such as vitality, perfect cellular function, love, money, peace, wisdom, good will, expansion, and creativity all create perfect health.

Reinforcing and expanding perfect health in any aspect of my life requires an attitude of gratitude for the Good flowing into my life and a consciousness of passing on the Good to other beings, no matter if the Good is money, love, good will, peace or any other expression. This attitude keeps the supply flowing, through me, revitalizing me, expanding me, and changing the consciousness in the world. The key is the continual movement and expansion of the flows of these life energies.

Healing is not about curing; it is about revealing a false belief and replacing it with a spiritual truth about the individual. Healing occurs in the mind. It is the healing of a perception.

Perfect health is always present in the Divine Mind of Spirit for an individual. It must be revealed in the mind of the individual before it can manifest in the body and affairs. To the degree perfect health is revealed and believed, it is also manifested to that same degree. "It shall be done for us as we believe."

Sometimes it is not easy for an individual to change their perception from the condition they see, to the spiritual truths regarding perfect health. When a person has a broken leg or a broken heart, it is difficult to not focus on the pain. There lies the challenges for the Spiritual practitioner, an individual licensed by a metaphysical church who completes prayer treatment for others.

First, the practitioner must perceive the client as a whole, complete, healthy person, in order to be able to do any good in treatment. That is all that is required for the treatment to be successful. If the client or friend, seeking prayer treatment, also sees himself or herself as a whole, complete and healthy person the treatment becomes that much more powerful.

Now, I believe the only thing which ever needs "healing" is the *perception* of the *need* for healing. This false perception comes from a consciousness of lack and separation. Lack and separation are not real conditions in themselves; instead they represent *illusions* of an absence of abundance and wholeness. The "healing" that needs to occur becomes the strengthening of the realization of abundance and wholeness. The healing requires my continual focus of energy, attention and intention on seeing the wholeness of being in every situation and every condition. In having a perception of wholeness, I automatically have the belief that every situation already is healed (and whole).

## My Healing Through The Use of Spiritual Principles
*"Happy" Shaw*

I was personally healed of my attachment to my childhood molestation victimization story by embodiment of several spiritual principles, not just one. If I were completely spiritually realized, I could have healed this situation by the use of the two principles: God is All and God is Good, but I obviously needed to work through this healing at different levels when I was ready to embody each of the Spiritual Principles.

Though I had an intense desire to heal this wound in my 20's, traditional therapy only seemed to make slight headway. Though the doctor released me from treatment after going over the molestation issue and others, I certainly didn't feel "well" with the molestation event. Later on in my life, every time I experienced a "betrayer" situation the same feelings of being violated would return, along with, in some cases, intense and unjust anger and overwhelming hurt beyond which would have been normally called for by the current event. Clearly showing the unhealed event of the molestation was still playing out in behavior patterns of my feeling abandoned, not good enough, unimportant and feeling I was always getting "screwed" in most relationships.

Though my desire for healing remained strong, and periodically, I would return to counseling in a one-on-one situation, I never seemed to be able to put this early wound to rest. I went for counseling for everything from an intense fear that my husband would die and I would collapse as a human being to problems with some members of an organization to which I belonged. Lots of on-the-surface stuff came up, but so many layers had been added to the original wound over the years that the counseling focus was often put on the current problem to solve it rather than working through the original problem. Though I was pronounced able to "cope," often that was about all I was doing and sometimes barely that.

My desire for complete healing eventually lead me into group therapy with women who had experienced similar child molestation, incest or rape events. Through the inner child work we did, I managed to clear out some of the old infection from the original wound. However, until I started attending a metaphysical church and studying spiritual principles I did not understand that it was not enough to clean out the wound. The false beliefs which had been embedded in my consciousness also had to be removed or dissolved.

I have read more books on healing and the release of old patterns that I can count. However, I will discuss several texts which have helped me recently and continue to help me in understanding spiritual principles and the creative process.

I was especially helped in dark hours by Melody Beattie's *The Language of Letting Go: Daily Meditations for Codependents*. Much to my surprise, I found out recently that while I had learned some of the lessons in this book, I had more to learn on a deeper level. I had recently confused standing up for myself with using anger to do it. So I hauled the book off my shelf and am reading it again. The Spiritual Principles in it are couched in modern language such as: "Letting Go in Love and Letting Go of Sadness."

As a child and young adult, I was programmed to believe that my feelings about this molestation incident did not matter and that it was best to put it behind me. Above all I was not to talk about it. This faulty reasoning led to an embedded false belief in my consciousness of "I don't matter because my feelings don't matter." Through therapy, I learned that my feelings were important and it was okay to express how angry I was that my body had been violated by someone I had trusted. Finally, today research is being done on the facts that children do molest other children and young teens also molest younger children.

In my forties, I found a cherub statuette at a garage sale. It had a male cherub looking sexually at the little female cherub. Though I was attracted to it enough to buy it, it also repulsed me.

During the stress of building of our new house in 1992, I begin to focus more and more on killing myself, but when we were ready to move out of our rental house into the new house we had built, I was determined I would not take with me the old feelings of hating myself and seeing myself as "bad." I took the cherub statue, a brown paper sack and a hammer down to the Rio Grande River.

There, I ranted and raved at the person who had molested me, put the statue in the brown paper sack and smashed it to bits with the hammer, finally crying and releasing some of the old anger. Then I threw the bag in the river, letting it go down stream. I started at that point to replace the false belief of "I don't matter and my feelings don't matter" with the true Spiritual principle "I do matter, for all is God."

The releasing of some of the anger about the original molestation act started healing a wound which had plagued me for over thirty years. Yet I still had a long way to go in single and group therapy after we moved in to the new house and lots of repeated pattern work to wade through, but I had at least made a start.

The second Spiritual Principle that helped to heal this wound was learning my Spiritual self is never damaged. In group therapy, I learned what had happened to me was not that unusual and that I wasn't *different*, *bad*, or *awful* because it had happened to me. I saw other women, who had experienced similar things in their lives, pick up the pieces and make something out of their lives now. I was encouraged to do the same. So the Spiritual Principle I eventually embodied here was "Spirit is Changeless."

The third Spiritual Principle I used to heal this wound was forgiveness. I realized the anger I held toward the molester and the people who wanted me to keep silent about it was only doing me harm and keeping me from living a life of peace. I forgave all the people involved in this incident and myself, knowing that all are expressions of God and that if I wish to receive forgiveness I must be the first to give it.

The Bible and other sacred texts are filled with stories of forgiveness, but what really seemed to clarify this principle for me was working with a children's book illustrator on a kid's book about Jonah and the whale. The illustrator, who had tried to retell the Bible story simply didn't get it at all – in my opinion. I started rewriting the story myself and uncovering its real secret. Jonah judged the people in the cities he wanted God to destroy and he was later judged in the same way by the sailors on the boat who threw him into the sea. I started to see how God's forgiveness really works. Jonah was awed by God's forgiveness for him. Then he was later able to understand how he must forgive the "wicked" people in the cities and help save them. Because God loved them just the way He loved Jonah. The rewriting of this "children's" story made me realize the loving God we talk about is *really in* the Old Testament if you really know how to read the stories metaphysically and apply them on a Spiritual level.

The fourth Spiritual Principle I embodied in this healing was that of love. I learned to love myself and the inner child within who was wounded; thereby, finally replacing my old false beliefs about myself with Truth. *I am lovable because I am part of God and God is Love.*

The text which has had the most profound impact of my understanding the creative process and the principle of love is a book for writers called **The Writer's Journey: Mythology for Screenwriters and Storytellers** by Christopher Vogler. This book is a concise and concrete study of Joseph Campbell's work on mythology throughout the world. It describes the hero's journey, which is really the story of any man or woman, who has a character flaw or false beliefs about himself or his self worth and who on his journey through life to reach his goals has to finally confront the dark side of himself. In this journey/life process, he learns to accept all parts of himself and learns that no matter what was in the past that he *now* has a choice to live out of love for oneself and others and that each person is responsible for creating or working out their own salvation.

The last time I was in my home state, about three years ago, I was able to hug the person who had hurt me and see him as someone new today and not the person who had molested me. He isn't *that boy* any more than I am still *that girl*. This is the embodiment of the Spiritual principle of forgiveness in action.

Please understand that I am not saying what happened to me was "right" or "good." It wasn't. It shouldn't have happened to me or to any of the other people who have been hurt in this manner. But it did happen and my challenge today is either to forgive and go on and live a peaceful life or surrender to living my life in "hell" forever by making my focus continually about what happened in the past.

After all the anger I carried with me for so long, it is, indeed, refreshing to have put most of this aspect of my life behind me. Though echoes still come up on occasion, I recognize them more readily now and deal with them more speedily. I am very grateful to have learned about the process of healing through Spiritual Principles and to now be equipped to realize when I *haven't fully* "let go and let God." When I come to the realization that there is more work to be done, I can then return to working on embodying more Spiritual Principles and put myself back in Spiritual balance. Spiritual balance, I believe, is the peace that passes understanding.

## Rediscovering Health
*Jeannie Bullard*

The process of healing treatment is always one of self-treatment. Healing is revealing, releasing, letting go. We are already the perfect pattern of health. All manifestation to the contrary is rooted in a distorted view or belief. Disease is self-inflicted through our limited thinking.

The body is the out-picturing of thought, an original Divine Thought now encrusted with human beliefs concerning limitation, hurt, pain, resentment, etc. Much like a ship's hull that over time becomes encrusted with barnacles, it can be returned to beauty by a time in dry dock (meditation) to scrape away the barnacles (release of negative thoughts). The body will reveal perfect wholeness if we liberate the mind from distorted thoughts. The mind must allow that which is not of Spirit to fall away.

The thoughts that distort and block the energy flow in our bodies are thoughts that perpetuate a sense of separation from our Source, the Divine Spirit. These thoughts construct shadow walls that divert the flow of perfect health. These are lies we have told ourselves concerning the nature of life. So any condition or disease is merely a thought or thoughts acting upon the body to out-picture as a physical mirror of our mind.

By returning to the conscious intelligence within we are restored and renewed by the realization of our Oneness with Spirit. We must turn away from appearances. Turn towards the Divine Reality, that great intelligence and harmony that constantly radiates order and balance throughout the body. The body is the malleable face of Divine Substance, sculpting Itself to our thoughts. Let the human mind be stayed on Spirit.

Healing is a remembrance – a recalling of the Truth – of our vital kinship with the ALL, a perfect realization of unconditional Love and Life. And "perfect love casteth out fear"– the fearful thoughts that mesmerize us into believing in separation. Fear and shadow dissolves in the illuminating light of revelation. The real body is spiritual and will conform to its perfect pattern if we turn our attention Godward.

We are now, this moment, a conscious embodiment of perfect health and balance. The body is the temple of Living Spirit which animates, sustains and rebuilds after Its own image. The Infinite Intelligence within each cell constantly maintains and renews. As the mind recognizes and beholds the Truth, the body will realign with its innate Divine Pattern.

### PRAYER TREATMENT

***Recognition:***

Spirit is all there is. God is complete wholeness, balance, perfection and health. From this Substance of formless perfection, all forms emanate. Spirit is First Cause, the constant creative principle that makes life out of Itself by becoming the thing it makes. God is the Perfect Pattern out-picturing all life.

***Unification:***

I am a unique creation of Spirit. I am made directly from God-Substance according to the perfect plan contemplated by the One Mind. I was invited into this world through the mind of God. I reflect all the Divine qualities of the Creator. <u>Insert Name of Person Requesting Prayer Treatment</u> is also made of God-stuff. Held as a thought in Universal Mind, he is known and loved completely. He enters life by special invitation as a manifestation of the perfection and glory of God.

***Realization:***

<u>Insert Name of Person Requesting Prayer Treatment's</u> body is the temple of Living Spirit. Spirit animates, sustains and rebuilds his/her body after Its own perfect image. The Divine healing agent within him/her knows only perfect health and harmony. The Infinite Intelligence within each cell is constantly maintaining and renewing. Divine Spirit radiates throughout his/her body. <u>Name</u> glows with the wholeness of God. The Perfect Pattern

manifests now. An emotional, mental and physical transformation is evident. The Love of God enfolds _Name_ and he/she bathes in perfect harmony and wholeness. Instantly he/she recognizes and accepts this Truth as his/her body realigns with its innate, spiritual blueprints. Balance and faith reflect in _Name's_ thoughts and feelings. He/she expresses the God-Self within him/her. Mighty currents of health wash over him/her in waves of perfection, love and light. All fear, stress and confusion is swept away in this crystal current. _Name_ feels a quickening. He/She is lifted into the light. He/She is illumined. He/She is healed of thoughts of separation as he/she becomes one with the Creator. He/She is refashioned. Divine Identity blesses him/her now and forever.

### *Thanksgiving:*

I praise joyously the life and health in every cell of _Name's_ body. I am thankful for the healing light that continually renews and rebuilds him/her after the pattern of Divine Perfection. I delight in the instantaneous evidence of good health. I am thankful for _Name's_ realization of perfect wholeness and wellness and his/her opportunity to express life's wholeness and balance.

### *Release:*

I release my word into the creative substance of the Law, knowing that it is already accomplished, I allow it to be and so it is.

# SECTION FOURTEEN

## The Perfection of Perceived Imperfection

*"If the doors of perception were cleansed everything would appear as it is, infinite."*
– William Blake

## got spirit?

## The Perfection of Imperfection
*Lynne Curtis*

In 1967 I was serving a tour as a Navy nurse in Adak, Alaska. The island had a 13-bed hospital where nurses alternated duty between the ward, the clinic and the delivery room. I felt one of the best parts of nursing was the reward given to the world after a long, hard labor, a fresh new life.

On one such occasion, I was working with a young woman having her first baby but whose labor had been stalled for a long time. The doctor, a wonderful young man from North Carolina, decided to give this woman a drug which strengthens the force of contractions and speeds up the labor. As was routine, I calculated the proper dosage to be given and checked my math with the doctor. She was to receive one tenth of a minim, but I picked up the wrong syringe and actually drew up ten times the amount and gave it to the patient.

In just a few minutes, the woman was crying out in pain as she began having one forceful contraction after another. In a few more minutes the contraction was continuous and the baby's heart rate began falling. The doctor asked to see the syringe I had just used and instantly realized the mistake. The woman was quickly becoming exhausted and hysterical, and the father was getting panicky.

The doctor quickly talked to the couple and explained that the baby was in trouble and a C-Section was needed immediately. I ushered the husband out of the labor room, called for help and wheeled the gurney into the delivery room already being prepared. I was extremely calm during this process and did what I needed to do to assist in the surgery. Within 30 minutes of the injection, the doctor was making an incision into the patient's abdomen. The baby's heart rate continued to decrease and was now below 100, an ominous sign for the infant,

When the doctor took the baby out of the uterus, it was not

## got spirit?

breathing and was blue. I felt helpless standing in the wings. Each of us in the delivery room were silently yelling, "Breathe, baby breathe!" I was terrified at the thought the baby might not live. For what seemed like hours, the doctor suctioned the infant, stimulated it and turned it upside down gently patting it over and over.

After a couple of interminable minutes, the baby gave a weak cough. With a little more stimulation, it was soon pink and wiggling and screaming its head off. I did what I needed to do to complete my duties, but when the Mom and baby were settled, I went to the lounge and fell apart. Tears streamed down my cheeks and I was doubled over in guilt and fear.

The doctor must have noticed me because he was soon at my side and listened as I blubbered out my sins over and over. "I'm going to quit nursing! I don't deserve to be a nurse! I'm unsafe. I've got to tell!" I do not remember all that transpired in those next few weeks and months. I spent a lot of time with the mother and baby who both did very well and was very grateful to those who had "saved her baby."

The doctor talked to me a great deal during those weeks and months about how I should not give up nursing – that I was a conscientious, caring and skilled nurse and many would suffer and lose if I left. I kept holding onto the notion that I needed to suffer, to pay for my mistake in some significant way. I have no idea where I would be today but for that doctor's kindness and understanding and lack of judgment. I remember him saying something to the effect, "I doubt that there is a single doctor or nurse who has chosen to truly engage in this profession who hasn't made at least one mistake that compromised a patient in some way or even caused a death. In order to truly be of service to others, we must let go of our need to be perfect, to always be right and somehow punish ourselves for our mistakes at the expense of our gifts."

That mistake happened over thirty years ago. I am still a nurse and have enjoyed a distinguished career. This incident has been a touchstone for me in my "growing up" process. In the *Course of Miracles*, there is a quote about our accepting our littleness as arrogance and not seeing ourselves as God sees us. That idea has haunted me since I first read it and I realize that in the weeks and months following this event, I truly believed my evaluation of me rather than God's. I believed that I was little, evil and bad. Many feelings arose during those critical weeks; I felt shame, guilt, secrecy, limitation and fear. I felt out of Integrity. I wanted to contract from life.

The doctor's questions bounced around in my head. "Suppose you do leave nursing, who will that serve? How many lives will be altered physically, mentally, spiritually if your unique gifts are lost?"

There are so many specific issues in this incident that could be addressed; truth, integrity, honesty, but I choose to focus on the bigger picture: the arrogance of holding onto the small self versus the wisdom of remembering the grandeur of my Higher Self. The truth is that for almost all of those years which have passed since I made that mistake I held onto my little self.

I was in my early twenties during this time and although I had a strong religious background, I was pretty much unconscious spiritually. The question of smaller versus larger self would never have occurred to me. For years I debated, "Should I have told the family?" It is a valid question. Would I have felt less guilt and served better if I had told?

To get an understanding of the larger picture, I want to address the feelings which arose for me. Shame was well known. I had worn its oppressive yoke all my life and felt its "you're not okay" as a constant companion. Secrecy was also worn comfortably. We were carefully taught to hide who we were behind bravado, righteousness, and the illusion that all was well. Limitation was translated as never enough: "I am not enough, what I do is not enough, what I think is not enough," and the family credo, "Be enough but don't be more enough than me."

Fear enveloped everything. Even God was a critical parent who judged everyone and everything and punished us for even eating meat on the wrong day. And what of guilt? Classically, guilt infers that "I am flawed, bad and not worthy and therefore, need to be punished."

Suppose we redefine guilt as an acknowledgment that our Higher Self is alive and well and that maybe guilt is a distress urging us to respond from the Higher Self. If guilt comes from that higher place, then the distress we feel is at not using the gifts we have and it becomes a betrayal of our Higher Self.

Then how am I using the term *arrogant*? It is lending importance to the little self. It is ignoring the grandeur of God in you and choosing to lament your littleness. And that is grandiosity of the subtlest kind. That is a cover-up for despair. It infers a reactive rather than a responsive approach to life and we begin to contract from the larger Self. Arrogance creates the illusion that we are somehow protecting ourselves from the big, bad world. It supports the concept of duality that "I am separate and need to hold onto my plans for how the world *should* go." This kind of arrogance appears to be expansive because it blows us up, but it actually results in a contracting away from our Higher Self. We say on one side of our mouths, "I am a God," and on the other side, we never even question our littleness

What did I actually chose to do thirty years ago? I chose not to tell. Was it right? I'm sure it's arguable. How did it change me? I became a more compassionate and caring person and I began to live more consciously. I became more human and accepted humanness in others, I used this experience as a teaching tool for my students. Did I skirt right and wrong somehow? Perhaps. Yet I felt incredibly humbled by this experience. I realize that prior to this, I was an arrogant nurse, because I grew up in a family in which arrogance was a survival technique and a substitute for true self value. Humility is usually perceived as diminishing us but it really expands the Self, for it comes from the realization of our connection to Spirit. It is a willing submission to be one with the Divine Will and is a peaceful state that exists in the Higher Self.

It is difficult to face the things we don't like about ourselves. Difficult challenges strengthen our survival skills. Our most profound fears deepen our faith. Weaknesses beckon us to grow and will not overtake us unless we surrender.

Nursing carries with it a big responsibility and therefore risk. If I had decided to quit nursing it would have denied the larger wisdom of my uniqueness and it would have been a diminishing of my Higher Self. I would have convinced myself that I and all that I am here to accomplish does not matter.

Instead, I became willing to live with imperfection, with uncertainty, with not knowing the bigger picture, with traveling with guilt long enough to get to the place that I would one day understand it, and to allow that a C-Section might have been part of the Divine Plan and not controlled by me.

It is very scary for me to let go of the reins and the illusion that I am somehow in charge, for it reminds me of the helplessness I felt in that delivery room so very long ago. It is an incredible realization for me of just how much meaning I have attached to this single event. Yet, as a result of it, I grew, I became more and I moved closer to becoming who I really am.

We are now celebrating a new millennium and thinking about making some changes, perhaps even moving toward our Higher Selves. There is nothing we need that we do not already have. It is arrogant to think that we must be more, do more or have more to be worthy of our desires. The grandeur of God is in each one of us and it is embracing our larger self to believe God's evaluation of our value.

## PRAYER TREATMENT

*Jeannie Bullard*

**Recognition:**

God is. God is all there is. God is the Living Source animating all life. Universal Mind is first cause, the Originator and all effect. Spirit is the constant, creative principle that becomes the thing It makes.

**Unification:**

God is my life. I am made from Spirit-Substance as a unique individualized contemplation of God. God expresses as me. I reflect the perfect life of God. Spirit is my identity.

**Realization:**

Suddenly, my eyes are opened. The scales of separateness fall away. Divine Love transforms my sight. Life is only one Being. I am one entity with all people. I am God expressing Divine Creativity as the human race. Every life is God walking on earth. I walk in common spirituality with All. I am God greeting God. I am centered in Oneness, Wholeness and Unity. From this center point of Divine Wisdom and Spiritual Sight, I embrace and embody the commonality of Universal Mind. Every idea is God expressing. Every religion, person, place, thing, idea is a facet of the one glittering jewel. I behold the spiritual man, the spiritual prototype of perfection. All my limiting perceptions are dissolved in the light of Truth. I am renewed.

**Thanksgiving:**

I am thankful for the gift of spiritual sight and the opportunity to view the world through God's eyes.

**Release:**

I release my word into the creative substance of Law, knowing that is already accomplished, I allow it to be and so it is.

**got spirit?**

*My Notes About The Perfection of Perceived Imperfection*

# SECTION FIFTEEN

## Practicing the Presence

*"Oh, Great Spirit, Earth, Sun, Sky and Sea,
You are inside and all around me."*

— Native American Chant

## Practicing the Presence
*Rebecca Hathaway Allen*

The Pentitente Indians wear horsehair vest as a sacred practice. The constant irritation of the vest is a reminder of the constant presence of God. That practice seems very sensible to me; I too need a constant awareness of the Presence.

Horsehair is hard to find and I would have no idea how to weave it into a vest. I thought of an alternative, not as dramatic as a horsehair vest, but effective, none the less. I have worn my watch on the right wrist, which is the opposite and therefore awkward wrist for me. This simple practice is a constant irritation, just like a horsehair vest. Every time I notice the odd sensation, I am reminded to notice the Divine Presence.

This has proven to be a wonderful discipline. The reminder arrives at just the correct moment. When I am pressured, rushed, and anxious about deadlines, I turn my attention to my watch. It is at just these times that I need the reminder to fall back into the Present.

I am also reminded that these moments are the creating "cause" of tomorrow. As I return to the Present, I consciously determine the "effect" I wish to create. It reminds me that I have an opportunity to consciously make a choice.

Time has taken on a different perspective. One day, I realized that in raising my hand to check the time, I was giving it an odd little salute. Do I choose to salute time? I think not. I do not choose to be ruled by Ol' Father Clock. I choose to be regulated by my own internal pulse. My pulse, the one that beats to the Infinite Beat, the pulse that is Ageless and Timeless, is the pulse that entrains with the Universal Time, which is the Heartbeat of God.

Frequent glances at my watch caused me to notice something else. If my attention is distracted from the Present for a split second, I am not giving those with whom I was speaking the recognition they deserve. I realize that God is not limited to me in this Present, those with whom I am speaking are also God in this moment. I don't want to be impatient with God. To give others my full attention is to be in the Presence of God.

Putting my watch on my right wrist has caused me to begin to be aware. I look at my watch and ask myself some quick questions. Am I being with God in a manner that is meaningful to me? Moreover, am I giving God a good time? As an expression of God I have an obligation to live with integrity, joy and love – am I taking the time to do that?

## The Art of Conscious Living
*Jeannie Bullard*

To be practicing the Presence means we must be on purpose, with intent, in the present moment. The Presence is available in the wholeness of the now. Our lives unfold one moment at a time, a bridge of timeless moments. If we are not present, fully in the moment, we are never aware of our lives or the gifts that are placed before us. Our lives are lost to us even as we are supposed to be living them. We wake up to Truth and find that we have not lived, or worse, that we have lived someone else's life because we did not have the awareness or discipline to experience our own.

The art of conscious living is simple and powerful. We capture our moments by stopping and being present, by removing all the extra ingredients inserted by our over-active, wandering minds. When we withdraw the negative thoughts that color the performance of a task, the task becomes pure action, a movement meditation, done for the pure expression of doing. The action does itself with effortless activity, and within the graceful celebration of now, the voice of God whispers. If we can hold the present moment in its fullness without imposing our ego self upon it, then we can observe its potential.

## Practicing the Presence by Ritualizing Mundane Tasks
*Jeannie Bullard, Happy Shaw, and Barbara Fox*

**Jeannie:** I find myself procrastinating paying the monthly bills, but once completed, there is a sense of satisfaction. I can diminish the procrastination by acting in the moment and not postponing and by meditating/concentrating on the satisfaction of completion. I can honor each company for extending credit or providing a service. Each check written becomes a celebration of abundance and tangible evidence of Universal Supply.

I can ritualize the process by adding an opening prayer of joy and abundance and close the task with a prayer of thanksgiving for all that has flowed through me to be distributed to others. I recognize the law of circulation as a power for good in my life. A prayer treatment for ever increasing abundance, visualizing my checkbook as a channel for God's good gifts could also be incorporated. Paying monthly bills can become a prayerful recognition that the Presence of God's Spirit is present in *every* task.

**Happy:** Since to me Practicing the Presence means feeling a sense of peace in my activities, I could choose to cook supper earlier in the day or in the morning first thing so that I don't feel rushed, overwhelmed or worn out at the end of my work day with one more task. I can also cook large meals which can be eaten for two suppers so that I don't have to cook every night.

I could make or buy a special apron to wear as I performed this task. It could be symbolic of a priestess's robe. I could bless myself as the person or priestess who has been given or who has taken on the responsibility for this important task.

I could place some water on the stove for a cup of tea for myself to drink in a quiet manner after the supper is in the oven. This tea could be a symbol of God's living water or Spirit.

I could remember that the food or the ingredients are provided by the Source and that plants and animals have given

# got spirit?

their forms so that I and my family might live in bodily form on this planet. I could give thanks to the Source of all by lighting a special, tall candle on my kitchen island, reminding me of the light of Spirit surrounding me and which lives in everything.

I could put on some beautiful, soothing music to make me feel peaceful as I set about this task. The music would be symbolic of hymns of praise to the Source of all.

I could turn in each of the four directions, blessing the Spirit within the farmers, producers and supermarket owners who have all played a part in raising and bringing this food to my home. At this point, I could light four more candles, one for each direction, and place them around my kitchen.

I could give thanks and bless my husband for working to bring in the money to pay for the food. I could place pictures (or visualize pictures) of my husband, daughters or anyone who would eat the meal and myself on my kitchen counter with the Source candle as I prepare the food to eat.

I could give thanks and bless my bowls, pans, pots and stoves and all the utensils I need to make the supper. I could arrange them all in a beautiful manner in my work area, having everything ready and organized from the beginning so that the task moves along without mishap or tension of having forgotten something.

I could think of my cookbook or recipes as "the principles" of cooking, knowing that the Universal law will use these ingredients like unformed substance to create forms like casseroles, meat loaf, or whatever. I could remember that on a microcosmic level I am revealing the Law of Creation.

I could place flowers on each person's tray or the table. Or I could use something else that is beautiful. I could spend some time arranging pleasant color combinations of dishes, napkins and silverware so anyone sharing the meal felt a sense of beauty while eating.

After I am finished in the kitchen, I could give thanks that the

# got spirit?

task was performed so effortlessly and beautifully. I could blow out each candle with a special prayer or phrase. Then I could put everything back in its place so it would be ready for the next time the task needs to be done.

My husband always says his doing the dishes is his contribution to the meal, but I could stack them neatly or put them in some water to soak, making his job easier. I could also remember to thank him for doing them or buy a special card to thank him.

Then taking my tea, I could move into a room with a beautiful view of the environment or imagine being in a beautiful meadow or looking at the mountains for a while before moving on into another activity.

**Barbara:** I find keeping track of my paperwork and records for Fox Productions one of my most difficult tasks. I believe this is a symptom of a false belief in consciousness, but regardless of the reasoning behind it, I recognize it as a circumstance in which I have great difficulty in seeing the face of God.

However, if I use my imagination, I can envision myself taking each individual document, receipt and canceled check statement and filing it as it comes. As I do this, I see the larger picture. My diligent, albeit mundane, work is a way of creating, yet another microcosm of the macrocosm of God. Since God is divinely ordered, so too, is my life. Each bit of filing I do reminds me yet again of this comforting truth. I recognize God as the Source of my income and supply, and freely, I circulate my talents and resources and they are circulated back to me in ever greater supply.

There is a two-fold benefit to this practice. Not only do I experience the joy of Oneness in yet another context of my life, I gain a greater financial freedom as I release the fears of not being organized enough when tax time comes around. All my papers are together, all my expenses tabulated, all my business mileage, medical expenses and gross receipts accounted for. With a push of a computer button, I am prepared to bring forth a complete set of financial records for my CPA to prepare my taxes.

This simple and practical way of practicing the presence brings me to an even greater level in the evolution of my business: with a firm sense of emotional security regarding my finances, I am now able to examine opportunities for business investments, in marketing and financing for expansion. Therefore I am free to negotiate confidently and effectively in all areas of my business, from a space of abundance, and to get the best deal possible. Pretty incredible return for practicing the presence in such a mundane endeavor!

## PRAYER TREATMENT
*Jeannie Bullard*

**Recognition:**

God is. God is all there is. Universal Mind, the Living Source, is the originator of all things. Every form flows from the One. Spirit is First Cause, the constant creative principle that makes life out of Itself by becoming the thing it contemplates. God is limitless, infinite, expanding life.

**Unification:**

I am a creation of God, made from God-Substance as a unique spiritual expression. Spirit made me out of Itself by direct contemplation. <u>Insert Person's Name Who Is Being Treated</u> also moves, lives and has his/her being as a thought held in Divine Mind. He/She is the perfect Spirit of God, contemplated by God as unique entities, directly formed from Universal Mind Substance. As a channel of Divine Intelligence, he/she is the living reflection of the Infinite.

**Realization:**

All life is perfectly orchestrated by Infinite Intelligence. The Presence within <u>Name</u> now manifests as right action, peace, harmony, and strength. Within Divine Mind there are no mistakes, no loss – only right and good completion. <u>Name</u> releases fear and resistance, letting God transform all into the perfect opportunity for love and for good. Now, a powerful flash of revelation illumines her/his mind. _Name_ realizes and accepts the Divine Plan of all life. He/She desires only what Spirit desires. He/She allows his/her own control and intentions to stand aside allowing the unconditional love and knowing of the One to flow through him/her as him/her. _Name_ expresses love and compassion as he/she shows up in the moment, acting as a caring, calm person. As part of the glorious harmony of the universe, _Name_ leaves the outworking of others' lives to Universal Mind. He/She allows the indwelling Intelligence within each person to follow its own choice. He/She recognizes and embraces the beauty and order of All. Spirit manifests the highest good, through divine channels at the right time. All is as it should be within the grand design of the ONE.

### Thanksgiving:

I am thankful for the eternal love and comfort of the Divine and for _Name's_ realization of the ONE LIFE and Its perfect plan.

### Release:

I release my word into the creative substance of the Law. Knowing that it is already so, I rest in the embrace of faith, allowing it to be, and so it is.

**got spirit?**

*My Notes About Practicing the Presence*

# SECTION SIXTEEN

## Present Moment

*"We cannot live a choiceless life.
Every day, every moment, every second, there is choice."*
– Ernest Holmes

## Healing Power of Living in the Present Moment
*Jeannie Bullard*

To reveal the healing power of living in the present moment, we are required to be on purpose, non-judgmental, and have our attention in the present – not in the past or future. It requires a recognition that our lives and our relationships unfold only in moments. And the moment can only be *now*.

Life is all about relationship. And we live life from moment to moment. Focusing our attention on the life we are experiencing right now is a simple and powerful tool to bring us back into alignment with our own wisdom, our inner being. Through living now, we can accept personal responsibility for the direction and quality of our lives.

Living each moment as it unfolds allows us to cultivate an intimate relationship by tending to it with care and discernment. If we are projecting future *what ifs*, or lingering in the past, the joy and love of the moment is lost. If we are not experiencing the now, we are never really *in* relationship but only dreaming of or remembering one.

If we diminish our awareness of the present moment, we become automatic and unconscious and this will direct the quality of our relations. In the past and future, we feel fragmented, in the present moment there is integration, unity and an intrinsic wholeness.

Living in the moment is the art of conscious living as we self-observe our attachments and reactions in the moment without likes and dislikes, projections or expectations. When we live our lives from the space of now, our moments are gentle, appreciative, healing and nurturing, revealing the soul of others as pure, unconditional love.

Practicing mindfulness in relationships allows us to step free from the self-imposed chains of impatience, criticism, low self esteem and other limiting thoughts. These chains have been forged in the past. In the present moment, the past has no reality.

Being in the present is simplicity itself. It is quieting the incessant flow of the mind, stopping and being present. We let go of wanting something else to happen, and take a simple, profound step toward being able to encounter what is here now. We can let things be and allow them to unfold in their own natural way. We can touch the present moment with harmony and sincerity and not allow it to slip away unnoticed and unused. We can appreciate the bloom of each moment, the bloom of love and the rare beauty of each person with whom we chose to share our moments.

Allowing a person to be who they are, to hear what they say, and witness their actions without coloring our perceptions of them with our own experience and expectation is the healing gift of living in the present. There is an inner peace in knowing that only this moment is fundamental to all things. In the purity of unformed Spirit, time does not exist, it is always the eternal now. And only in the moment can compassion, beauty and love be revealed.

Stillness, wisdom and spiritual insight arise from the completeness of the present moment. Living in the now can be a delicate balancing act between the outer and inner worlds. It is accomplished through the voluntary simplicity of surrender to the Divine. As we are open and receptive, all time folds into the present moment. What will come next will be determined by what we are now.

Let the next moment arrive saturated in grace, unfolding naturally from the pure heart.

## Living in the Moment
*Dave Schultz*

We know we are living in the moment when three elements are present. Those elements are Consciousness, Connection, and Surrender. Consciousness means that we are paying total attention to where we are, what we are doing, and how we are feeling. We are totally focused on our experience of the moment. Connection means we have made an emotional connection to something or someone else. The *else* could be another human, a stranger, a tree, the still small voice within, or God. Surrender means that we let go of trying to control or resist outcomes, judgments or expectations of whatever we are engaged in. We are only interested in experiencing whatever is happening in the moment.

Living in the moment, or living in the now, as it is sometimes stated, is available to us anytime and anyplace. We don't need anyone else's permission or cooperation to live now. We don't even need to be in the same physical space with someone, in order to have a meaningful experience with him or her. We can truly be living in the moment, making it our present reality, over the phone with someone.

Why do so few people seem to have so few experiences where they are consciously living in the present moment? Apparently, few people in the modern world experience living in the present moment. They are always living their lives today as if they were still breathing in the past. Even when they do experience the sense of actually being alive in the present moment even by accident, they aren't aware of what just happened. They just know that something intimate and wonderful just happened.

Today, many people seem to live together in relationship to others as unconnected, unconscious, and certainly not in surrender to the moment or to each other. We have created large separations between our spiritual selves and our everyday lives.

Relationships are the laboratories to practice and express who we really are and why we are in this life.

The primary love relationship with another person is one of the most intense of these laboratories. Within that relationship, a person has the opportunity to reveal parts of himself that few other people see, or maybe he, himself, is unaware. Some parts may have been hidden to him for many years because of past painful experiences. However, this new primary relationship can be a vehicle for tremendous physical, emotional and spiritual healing.

In order for healing to occur, there must be moments where both are living in the same present moment. Moments where the walls between two people are taken down and the separation between them evaporates. There is no judgment, obligation or expectation; there is only acceptance and recognition of the human-ness of each other. In that safe bubble of suspended time, Truth comes more easily and defenses seem unnecessary.

With the unconditional love and acceptance of another person, one more easily accepts and forgives himself. In that moment of living in the present, healing occurs.

## Healing Power of the Present
*Barbara Fox*

The value of living in the present moment to all relationships is priceless. Ideally, we should be present in every moment we live, but with life maintaining an ever-increasing pace, we rarely are. However, in a spiritually-realized life, we can be focused, present and fully feeling all the moment has to offer, whatever the emotions.

There are numerous benefits of living in the present moment, but I would like to recognize two, which are of exceptional healing value: dealing with the present in the present and transmutation of unfinished past issues.

Dealing with the present in the present is something many of us forgot how to do when we were busy trying to survive our childhood. Those who come from incest or another kind of abuse background know this all too well. As children, the experiences we dealt with were often so overwhelming, we could not process them and stay sane. So we suppressed, fragmented or forgot them by blocking them out of our consciousness. Imagine a little girl or boy having to reconcile that a parent is beating them or sexually exploiting them while the child must continue to look to its parents as the source of food, clothing and shelter. Abused children's chief means of survival would most likely be to live in their imagination, a place where they could create a life where their parents were kind and loving and they felt safe. As adults, these children will be challenged with finding healthy relationships while their primary impulse is to re-create dysfunctional relationships similar to that experienced with their parents.

In order to heal, we must remind ourselves it is a natural state to stay in the moment and that the coping skills, which may have gotten us through childhood, were not natural behaviors and they are not helpful now in our present life.

Through prayer treatment, we know the value of the present

moment as the point of power. The more we allow ourselves to stay in the present moment, the faster our process in healing will be. Feeling all of the moment in the moment decreases the creation of additional emotional baggage by immediate attention to the issues at hand. As a result, life is more current, and we are more likely to act on life rather than react to it.

Additionally, the more we allow ourselves to be in the present moment, the more we will begin to see the transmutation of unfinished business from the past. Being in the present moment reminds us of our true humanity. At first, the intensity of being truly present in the moment may be overwhelming and frightening to one who has suppressed feelings for nearly a lifetime. However, through courageous persistence, we will gradually adjust our perception to these present moments. They will begin to feel good as our internal "homing devices" recognize that present moments are experiences, which facilitate our creative self-expression. An alchemical process begins to take place in which these positive experiences begin to heal the tears in the fabric of the heart. We learn to trust more, feel deeply, and experience more completely the times of our lives. In this way, we are not just learning a new skill by living in the present moment; we are seeing how these "real time" moments themselves catalyze a healing within the individual.

A Universal Principle or Law (sometimes called a mental equivalent) can be used to affirm trust in our healing process such as: "Principle is never bound by precedent." Understanding that healing is the natural order of life, we come to understand that we can have what we have never had, we can know what we have never known and we can be what we, until now, never have been, simply by changing our core beliefs and replacing them with Spiritual Truth.

To one who has lived on the sidelines of life, the intoxicating nature of living in the present moment is strong enough to convince even the most ardent skeptic. I know this because it is the truth for me. Were it not for learning to be in the present moment with sponsors in Twelve Step recovery programs, metaphysical religious practitioners and other enlightened people, I doubt I would be pursuing my wildest dreams and desires today.

# SECTION SEVENTEEN

## Compassion

*"The way to do is to be."*
— Lao Tzu

## Do No Harm
*Lynne Curtis*

One of the directives of the Hippocratic oath is: "Above all, do no harm." I know what that means in medicine but I have come to learn what it means in relation to daily living. I am going to share a story about myself that has contributed greatly to my awareness and the evolution of my soul.

But first I'd like to share with you what led me to have this awakening. Sometime ago, I was reading Pema Chodron's book *When Things Fall Apart,* and the chapter was entitled "Not causing harm." In it she said: "Underneath our ordinary lives… there is a fundamental groundlessness. It's there bubbling… and we experience it as restlessness and edginess. We experience it as fear."

She suggests that we cause harm to others by not sitting with this groundlessness and becoming mindful. By practicing mindfulness we learn the art of refraining from reacting or acting out of habit. This groundlessness is a case of the "jitters" and it prevents us from ever relaxing.

Near the same time, I was reading in Joel Goldsmith's *The Thunder of Silence* a chapter about karma, also known as the Law of "as ye sow, so shall ye reap." Goldsmith writes: "The only way to stop sowing is to recognize our Spiritual Identity," and he adds, "and watch what wonderful ways the Father has of providing for us…"

These ideas hit me like a thunderbolt. I felt like Saul being knocked from his horse. So now, the story I promised.

As a result of some hellish experiences as a child, I got sex and love all confused. In my relationships with men I somehow got the idea that I couldn't be loved if I wasn't sexual. When a man was interested in me, I would soon feel a compulsion to be sexual so I could feel loved whether this man was the right one for me or not. I realized that a belief about myself rose from this need. *I believed that I needed someone outside myself to validate that I was lovable.* So if a man was nice to me, I began fantasizing that this was the relationship of my dreams! But another belief was also at play – *I'm really scared to be in relationship too.* So, not surprisingly, I attracted men who were not available in one way or another. But since I'm a moral person, I wouldn't think of "stepping out of line" and overtly pursuing someone. *Ah, but energetically, now that's another story.*

Energetically, on the most subtle of levels, I would:
1. find ways to be indispensable and always there for him thus enhancing my appeal by providing a subtle contrast of what he is missing in his own relationship
2. reach out, scheme, plot, plan and desire as much of him as I could and still rationalize my "purity"
3. and lastly, and perhaps the most damaging point, in focusing totally on this relationship, I would close myself off to all the other relationships that the Father might have in store for me

Soon this same scenario began repeating itself with a man who was "unavailable" but who was consistently there. I knew he had a partner so I was emotionally removed at first. Yet, over time I found myself becoming very attracted to him. Each time I develop a "crush" on someone, I struggle with appropriateness. I begin to compartmentalize what is spiritual and what is human. If my feelings overwhelm me, I find myself labeling them as "bad." I wanted his companionship, attention and friendship but I also wanted an intimacy that was not his to give nor mine to desire. We were having an emotional affair if not a physical one. I felt groundless. I felt edgy and restless, and a part of me was reaching and grasping for him, so I wouldn't have to feel alone, or unlovable or undesirable. Even though I was feeling out of integrity about spending more and more time together, I didn't want to change it.

As Stephen Levine says in *Who Dies?* "…desire… narrows the mind's capacity. It causes the mind to contract… satisfaction only occurs in the moving from not having to having."

When I was soul-searching about my participation in this

relationship, I could see just how my mind was contracting down on what this relationship was, or could be, or should be. I had very little room for anything else. I felt obsessed. I felt like a sandwich bag filled with water that was being compressed by some imaginary force. If I speak of my feelings, I would have to risk his not liking me anymore, or rejecting me, or even of being angry with me for upsetting the status quo. And God forbid that I have to deal with anyone's anger! If I told him of my feelings, I would also have to refrain from the activities I had come to treasure. I would have to settle into groundlessness. I would have to sit with my restlessness and my fear that he may not love me. As Chodron also said, I would have to relate to "the bubbles, burps and farts, all the stuff that comes out and expresses itself as uptight, controlling and manipulative behavior."

I remembered another quote by Goldsmith in *Practicing the Presence*: "...the very moment we have God, we have all there is in the world. There is no such thing as God and..."

I was so uncomfortable that I had to find a way to be at peace with my desires yet feel in integrity, too. I called him and asked if we could talk. The attraction I felt had grown out of proportion because it was unexpressed and I realized we couldn't be intimate when we're holding secrets. I wanted to back out up until the very second we began our dialogue, but I wanted to harm no one even more.

When we resist feeling our groundlessness, our desires and wants create a craving for any experience that will satiate us. We imagine some person, some car, some jewel, some house will put an end to our unquenchable thirst. We engage in fantasy and illusion and the "innate spaciousness that is our mind," as Levine calls it, is squeezed out of us. We then begin to identify with the object of our attention and mistakenly believe that "I am this desire," "I am this object," and "I am this thirst." The more we contract around the desire, the more we shut ourselves off from the flow of Truth and we really do "lose our minds."

This is called *suffering, or pain, or bewilderment or confusion* among others. We lose our sense of direction. We can't see the big picture because our awareness is so focused around one object. We yearn to experience some previous pleasure and enter into what Levine calls the "if only" realm. "If only I won the lottery… If only I had him, or her, or the job, or the car, everything would be okay." Our whole experience appears to become one of incompleteness and lack. Not surprisingly then, we become a magnet for more lack, more wanting, more insatiability and less availability for being in the present moment. Whether our desire is for sex or for happiness, the result is the same – we sacrifice wholeness for "something else." Just how much of our life is live in this kind of compulsiveness, pulled from moment to moment like some magnetic robot? Prisoners of our desires rather than choosers from a flow of unceasing possibilities.

I noticed that the more I desire him, the more pain I was in for the very nature of wanting is a feeling of incompleteness, of not having. An impatient waiting for another moment of satisfaction.

The bizarre thing about desire is that bubbling just beneath the surface is Infinite Expansion, Desirelessness, Satisfaction, Joy, Peace, Clarity and Wholeness. Satisfaction is the momentary experience of the vastness that lies beneath. Peace is experienced not because we get what we want but because for a moment desire does obstruct the joy and peace of our underlying nature. The second that desire disappears, we experience Desirelessness, we experience the Oneness in all Its Completeness. The paradox of all this is that our desires can lead us to Infinity but focusing on them from a state of mind "in lack" will block our having what we want.

During the talk with my male friend, I sat in my groundlessness and got still. I consciously chose to stop sowing a discordant relationship. I realized that my feelings were real but that the relationship that I was seeking was out of *sync* with the one that was before me. I wanted wholeness rather than the fragments I was accepting just so I wouldn't have to feel lack anymore. Despite the "jitters," we were both feeling, I experienced more intimacy than I had ever known and the relief was immediate. I felt at peace. I felt in integrity and I was able to keep my heart open in the process. I realized that I had achieved my deepest wanting: to know that a man can love me deeply, *and I don't have to be sexual inappropriately!*

About this time, I read something by Ernest Holmes, the author of *Science of Mind* that really affected me. In SOM he wrote: "Does the thing I wish to do express more life, more happiness, more peace to myself and at the same time harm no one?"

*Damn!* I didn't want to think about being *wrong, or selfish, or doing harm*. I wanted to keep the sweetness I felt. I liked the attention. I liked feeling special. I liked someone wanting to be with me. I rationalized that because I've been a good girl all my life, I deserved these few minutes of "harmless fun." After all, if you're not sleeping with someone, it's harmless, right?

But, with all this talk of *sowing, harming, reaping and refraining,* what was the real truth? This "romance" was an illusion! The emotional affair we were having was detrimental to him, to his partner and to me. I was not experiencing more life, more happiness, and more peace. I was going nuts! I felt selfish. I thought about what I was sowing for the relationship I wanted down the road. I thought about how I would feel if I were his partner and he was spending so much time with me. And I also relished the times we went for walks, or went to the aquarium or the zoo. But it was like trying to hold hands with a shadow and just as empty considering what I really desired in a relationship.

I was in the twilight zone of groundlessness. Groundlessness is that uncomfortable place where fear resides. I was afraid to give up what I had in my fantasy because I didn't know how to replace the feelings with something as sweet. So I was experiencing an anxiety born out of not feeling that I was currently safe, or lovable, or desirable. I was running around in circles searching desperately for a way to distract myself. I wanted my own relationship and was feeling an incredible impatience with not having it now. It caused me to speed up my life with more talking, more acting, running, jumping, dancing or just about anything that would help me not feel the pain of lack, or confusion, or edginess. This wanting stirred my passion, aggression, ignorance, jealousy and pride, emotions which, when not addressed, lead to overeating, overworking, over smoking, over drinking or over seducing. As Chodron said; it drove me into an "entertainment mentality."

Through my earnest soul searching, our relationship has changed. It is rich, lighter and more honest. I trust him and I trust me with him. I love his willingness to allow me to be neurotic, and compulsive for it also allows me to be authentic, expansive and imperfect. The compulsive feelings are gone because I no longer create expectations that squeeze my reality into a bag. I leave his relationship to him, for it is none of my business. I no longer try to reap something that isn't mine to reap. The chemistry is still there but I use the energy of it to stack onto what God has in store for me at the expense of no one. I feel a new love for myself growing out of a willingness to harm no one and to look at myself honestly and gently. I feel more willing to explore the dark side of myself rather than remain ignorant, and interestingly, it is liberating me!

## got spirit?

*My Notes About Compassion In My Life*

# SECTION EIGHTEEN

## Purpose

"Work is love made visible."
— Kahlil Gibran

## Purpose
*Barbara Fox*

I embarked on a program of spiritual study to gain insights that might lead me to become the kind of calm, poised, spiritually centered people I saw in church who always seemed so centered, so peaceful and happy! I wanted that. With all the internal work I had done, I still felt so much anxiety and difficulty with old beliefs. It appeared to me that certain people really walked the talk. They seemed to really know that all was well. I had read about it, I had heard about it, but I had never really felt it. I hoped that by committing myself to disciplined spiritual studies, I too would enjoy such a sublime way of life.

To a degree, I have achieved my goal but not without paying a price. During the course of my studies, I received word that I would be faced with losing my beloved job. I had the option of choosing a far less satisfying configuration of duties with substantially lower pay, and I felt torn. This was the work I had loved and done successfully for fourteen years, but all the studying I was doing was revealing a truth I could no longer ignore: I had to remain true to my inner self, even if it meant losing the job. What they were asking for was completely unacceptable. Then again so was unemployment!

This was the first place where I had to put faith to the test. If circumstances were indeed no longer appropriate for me to continue working at my job, could I dare to believe that God would bring me something better to take its place? I simply couldn't imagine anything better or more satisfying than working on the radio.

This was when the rubber met the road. If what I wanted was to have the kind of serenity I saw in others, I had to demonstrate the kind of faith that they had in the Universe to take care of them. It was totally foreign to truly believe in my heart that God really wanted what was best for me, and that we live in a Universe that gets its greatest glory when we heed our still small voice. Could this really apply to me too? This was a radical supposition that tried all of my old beliefs and perceptions of the world and catalyzed the transformation that I desired.

It has been through this singular challenge that I have had my greatest applied growth. I now have a home studio, and several promising leads. Plus, I was hired to do the audio books for the American Girls Collection. All this has given rise to an even greater awareness.

I have realized that I want to have a focus on giving young girls an edge in today's society – an edge I wish I had had but didn't. The power of the media to dictate standards of living, of physical beauty, of what's just plain 'right' was stronger than anyone cared to believe when I was growing up. Today it is much slicker and more persuasive and we have been exposed to it for so much longer that the brainwashing is nearly automatic. Young American women and girls are taught that sexuality is power, that breasts give them validity, and medically enhanced breasts open doors their intellect cannot.

Women are given the message that unless we are thin, we do not have representation (how many credibly overweight people are hawking products or on TV?). It is subtle, it is pervasive and it is deadly. Anorexia nervosa currently affects five to ten million females. This suffering is not due to a lack of available food, it is due to a lack of spiritual nourishment. Somewhere along the line, these girls received the message that they were not acceptable as they were. This must change if we are to evolve as a society.

I believe that my unique challenges as a woman in recovery from an eating disorder, low self esteem and incest give me a natural focus in this area. I know what's missing. I have suffered its absence, grieved its loss and raged over the injustice of not getting what I needed. All this has engendered in me a drive to give that which was missing for me, to others who are suffering similarly. It is cathartic. It is constructive. It feeds my soul.

I believe that my disciplined spiritual studies have awakened in me a greater awareness of the alchemy of soul healing. It would have been quite easy to remain a bitter victim of injustice. Instead, I can see how my experiences can benefit others. This is truly transcendent and I feel one of the purest expressions of the God within. It is like the blade of grass that breaks through the concrete sidewalk. Life is bursting forth, regardless of any seeming attempts to contain it, control it, or put it down.

I still have a long way to go. The mundane tasks of making cold calls and waiting for the phone to ring so I can do my wonderful work can still wreak havoc with my self esteem. I have periods where I doubt whether Spirit really is the lavishly abundant essence we all say it is. After all, grains of sand may be everywhere, but the balance in my checkbook does not appear nearly as infinite. After paying homage to the god of television, I have learned to put a great deal of stock in manufactured visual images.

However, when I turn my focus back to the Spiritual Truth, I am reminded that the physical world is simply the effect of thought. My intellect has grasped the concept, but sometimes there continues to be a little girl within who is very affected by what she sees. Now I know it is up to me to give that little girl every opportunity to see the truth of what it is instead of what others have told us to believe. So far, so good. And there is much, much more to be done.

## PRAYER TREATMENT
*Jeannie Bullard*

### For the Ongoing Unfoldment and Achievement of My Life's Purpose

***Recognition:***
Heavenly Mother/Father God, I know that you are all there is in the Universe. Spirit essence is the all of creation. It is the stuff of thought, word, and deed, the substance of all things large and

microscopic. All that exists is composed of this primary element of Spirit. Spirit by design is perfect, whole and complete. Spirit is pure love and joy, ever striving to become more of itself by becoming the things it creates. Spirit is all knowing and ever changing, yet its basic essence is changeless.

### *Unification:*

And I know that I am One with Spirit. I am made of the stuff of Spirit and, as such have the same attributes as my nature. I am inherently perfect, whole and complete, with an unchangeable core of pure love and joy and an ever-growing need to express my God-self more fully by becoming more in the image and likeness of Spirit. While I am forever changing, my basic Godhood cannot be altered.

### *Realization:*

And so I accept the truth of my being with open arms. I am a beacon of peace, light and hope; a walking embodiment of God's individuated expression as me, in as authentic a manner as I can be. This is my natural state. I flow most easily and effortlessly when I follow this true lead of my heart. I am divinely guided to circumstances that expand this idea in my consciousness and express this aspect of God in physical form. This is my birthright and in so recognizing it, I experience the deep peace that comes from living my truth.

### *Thanksgiving:*

I am deeply thankful for the knowledge of the truth of my being. I rest comfortably in the arms of God, knowing that these impulses toward greater self-expression are nudges from Spirit and I am grateful for them. I know that what I speak is already manifest in the mind of God,

### *Release:*

And so I release these words to Spirit knowing they must always manifest, for that is Law. And so it is, and so I let it be. Amen.

## Reflections On My Life's Purpose
"Happy" Shaw

During my spiritual studies, a visual image came to me of the shooting game played at a target range or at the fair, where a target is painted and shaped in the appearance of an "enemy." Once one has hit the target and knocked it down, it is very clear that there was no enemy at all. There was nothing of substance behind the painted picture – it was only an illusion, an illusion created in one's own mind.

So many of my old beliefs about myself and life and God and my relationships to others have come crashing down during these years of spiritual study just like this 'target' image in the shoot game. Once the illusions created by my false beliefs were shot through with Spiritual Truth, they fell and were shown to be just so much mistaken thought or false beliefs – or mirages.

We all have our "monsters," the things we make up to be afraid of. I especially like following passage which explores this idea of our home grown monsters.

"…he never either deceived or was deceived by the illusions of mass-suggestion. Whatever his taste in monsters, he never saw before him a many-headed beast. He only saw the image of God multiplied… Yet here was a detached and separated man, who ultimately loved God and God's creatures so much he completely forgot himself. To be objective, in the way I mean it here, is to live for the sake of others, to live effectively (even if strangely), to live responsibly so as to give more than we exploit, exhaust or oblige others. This St. Francis did with passion." Chesterton, 1957.

I especially like the idea in the Chesterton quote of St. Francis forgetting his taste in monsters and only seeing God multiplied. As we go through our lives, day-to-day, meeting but not recognizing God in form, if we can not forget out taste in monsters, we aren't coming from a God-centered place when we are looking at others, situations or events. And we are not able to control our need to *fix them* which is constantly rising forth from the little self and not from the God-Self that knows that all is already perfection.

If I feel I *need* to do something to or for anyone, then the little self is involved and is judging the appearances of a situation or people or relationship. It is always God Spirit who is doing the work of moving people toward recognizing their own perfection.

This does not mean we should not help others. We simply must discover what is motivating us. The *Course in Miracles* indicates that true giving is done out of an overflowing sense of our already having whatever it is we are wishing to give. When we are being Love or Being God in the World, seeing as God sees, we can give love. When we are being abundance Itself, we freely give abundance. The widow who gave her mite in the Bible gave out of a feeling of gratitude of what she had not because she felt the need to fix anyone else's circumstances. She gave from a simple knowing of "God has given to me and therefore, I give to others."

"Realizing that you may, in your ignorance, have been using the power of your mind negatively (not because you were evil but because of human ignorance, superstition and fear, which, to a certain degree, permeates every man's thought) you are not going to condemn yourself or anyone else because of this. If the light has come, the thing to do is to use it, forgetting the darkness." Ernest Holmes, *This Thing Called You*, page 128-129.

This passage sparks thanksgiving and gratitude within me of being included. In other words, it is not just me who has allowed negative thoughts to impress images that I do not want into Universal law. Dr. Ernest Holmes says that to a certain degree this has happened to everyone and that we are not to condemn ourselves or others for it. This is truly one of the greatest Spiritual passages I have ever read, as it indicates that no one need assume a moral superiority within themselves or with others.

From this passage, I realized that forgiveness often goes hand-in-hand with having judged something or someone in the first place as "wrong" or "evil" and that forgiveness happens within ourselves not outside of us. We usually make judgments out of a sense of fear. However, God holds nothing against us and neither should we hold anything against ourselves or any other person.

It doesn't mean that we don't chose our friends or the people we most enjoy being with or that as adults we allow ourselves to be abused, it is just that we all have our own "little Hitler" as Elizabeth Kubler-Ross calls our shadow side. So there is nothing in us that has a moral right to judge anyone else. And we are not to judge our little selves either because we allowed ourselves to be misguided for a time by superstition, ignorance, or fear. The important thing is that once we are awakened ("the light has come" in Dr. Ernest Holmes' words), we should make use of now being awake and forget and forgive where we once were.

This insight flows into that of the Prodigal Son from Luke in the Bible. It is a stunning insight that God sees no difference in the man who has been eating bean pods with the swine – and that that man is me.

I can now look back at my own "mistakes" and see them as moments that were just as sacred and important a part of my spiritual path as when I remember to return to Spiritual balance. For there is a knowing even within man as he partakes of the swine food and has it smeared on his face that he is loved even then and can return to knowing and basking in that Supreme Love. If this spark of Knowing were not already there, none of us would come to healing.

Over the course of my spiritual studies, I have changed from a person who didn't remember what it meant to be in the Presence to one who has so intensely felt the Presence that I glowed to the point other people noticed the light radiating from me. I have changed from a person who didn't want to do any work in the emotions because I was afraid of how painful it would be or of what I might find still in there to a person who has called a spiritual practitioner to help me finally remove some dregs of resistance to the Truth of my own Being.

## got spirit?

I have downsized my business, knowing that I only need the right clients to have abundance, not more of them. I have come to a place of knowing that I am being guided by God Spirit when I turn to God Spirit. However, even when I do not make a conscious effort to return to balance, I have such a powerful attraction to Spirit that It pulls me toward the Spiritual life in spite of any human resistance I might temporarily throw up in front of It.

Though I have not completely "named" what final occupation in which I will express myself and the new Spiritual insights I have gained, I do know that this occupation is being created for me and when it arrives I will recognize it and know what to call it. However, I have made a commitment to continue to learn more about who I am and my relationships to others through God-Self and through additional discovery of the Truth within me. I will create an even more Spirit-Centered life and an even more loving and supportive relationship with myself and others because I now have set my intentions to have those aspects in my life.

My unfolding purpose also continues to include the letting go of all past patterns which have operated negatively in my life. Doing so, I will move forward with my life into an even brighter radiance, healing, confidence and trust in myself and in God beyond any I have ever known. Thus, I will live a life of authenticity.

My personal intention is to open myself to Spirit's expressing Itself in all areas of my life through me, as me, and to learn to listen and view others without judgment or the need to correct them or fix the situation, as everything is perfect in Spirit.

## PRAYER TREATMENT
### "Happy" Shaw

***Purpose:*** for the on-going unfoldment and achieving of my Life's Purpose

***Recognition:***

God is Love. God made the entire Universe out of Itself, unfolding through Love. God simply makes up everything. And everything has a cast of love around it.

***Unification:***

Everywhere I look I see God unfolding. Even in the mirror. God smiles back at me as me. I am part of God. God is Love. I am part of God. And so God loves me. Not just a little, God's love flows over me and through me and around me as limitless Love.

***Realization:***

Because God loves me, I can love myself. Because I love myself, I can love others. My life purpose unfolds through my loving myself and others. My life purpose is an unfolding of God's love in the unique expression of me as me. God has been and continues to prepare me to express God's love through myself for all of Its creation at all times.

***Thanksgiving:***

I give thanks for the on-going unfoldment of God's love through me and through each person, creature, thing and event manifested on this plane we call the visible Universe. I give thanks that we can see and feel the Universe's beauty and know inside ourselves that it was created for us by Love, through Love, and out of Love and is to continue to unfold forever through unconditional Love. I give thanks that I am a part of Love's unfoldment in every area of my life and my purpose in living is filled with knowing, accepting and showing God's love.

***Release:***

So these Truths are and so I let them be.

# SECTION NINETEEN

## *Wholeness*

"The message we hear from all sources of truth is clear. We are all one. That is a message the human race has largely ignored. Forgetting this truth is the only cause of hatred and war, and the way to remember is simple: Love, [in] this and every moment."

– His Holiness the Dalai Lama

## The Perception of Wholeness
*Tammy L. Young*

Spiritual healing is rising above the appearance and realizing the spiritual truth of the condition we thought needed healing. We are actually realizing that there is no healing necessary because – in Spirit – there is nothing to be healed.

We know that Spirit is One, Complete, and Whole in and of Itself. There can be no fragmentation in Spirit and there is nothing which exists outside of the wholeness of God. Drawing on the qualities of Sprit, we can know that within this wholeness is Divine Love and Law, Abundance, Freedom, Joy, Wisdom, Perfect Health, Divine Right action, Divine Resolution, and Absolute Perfection.

When we are doing prayer treatment for ourselves or someone else, this perception of wholeness is enough to heal. Since we do not really heal conditions, but the false beliefs behind them, we can eliminate any false belief by replacing it with the awareness of wholeness.

The Spiritual Master, Jesus, clearly had a consciousness of wholeness. He performed miracles because he knew that everything was contained within the Wholeness of the Universe. He did not need to use denials and affirmations or any fancy technique because he instantly knew that there was nothing lacking and nothing sick in Spirit.

### PRAYER TREATMENT
*Tammy L. Young*

There is one Divine center of all reality. At this center exists all Life, all Love, all Intelligence, all Prosperity, and all Wisdom. This reality is God. God is the Source of all there is. God is the sustaining Power of the Universe. There is nothing outside of God for God is all there is.

I live and move and have my being as one expression of this

Divine reality. God is the source of my being and all that I am is God. I am one with God and one with Life, Love, Intelligence, Prosperity, and Wisdom. With every breath I take, I breathe in the essence of my being, God. With every beat of my heart, I am reminded of the Power which is God within me, as me.

I have a deep, abiding faith in the Power and Presence of God in my life. Spirit flows through me freely and powerfully as I am an open vessel for the expression of all that God is. I am a powerful person with many gifts to offer. God in me hears my inner desires and my intuition guides me to be what is needed for each individual and situation which comes into my life. I easily establish a loving, beneficial rapport and communicate the Divine message Spirit sends them through me. Spirit guides me to the perfect demonstration of Its work in the world.

My heart is filled with Joy and Thanksgiving for knowing the perfection of my relationships. I give thanks for this teaching and for the movement of Spirit within me which continues to lead me forward on a path of awakening. For the many gifts in my life I say, "Thank you God in me!"

I release these words now into the Law of my being, knowing that as I have spoken them they have already been manifest. I let go of them now as I release the very need to have spoken them. And so it is. And so I let it be. Amen.

**got spirit?**

*My Notes About Wholeness*

# SECTION TWENTY

## The Prodigal Son As Our Story

*"And he rose up and came to his father. And while he was yet at a distance, his father saw him and had compassion on him, and he ran and fell on his neck and kissed him."*

– Jesus, St. Luke 15:20

## The Prodigal Son As My Story
*"Happy" Shaw*

### The Two Sons

Just as almost everyone else does, I have a perceived duality of my "good" side and my "shadow" side. As a little child brought up in a fundamentalist church, I was taught to believe that this "shadow" or "sinner" side of myself was evil, and I was terribly afraid of it and the "Devil" who was supposed to tempt us to do evil. But I was even more afraid of God. God was the scariest thing I could imagine because he wiped out folks with floods and famine and killed people with lightening bolts and sent them to hell.

When my younger sibling was born, I was basically set aside and experienced abandonment feelings along with guilt and anger. Since I was never taught how to deal with "negative" feelings, I was convinced by four years of age that because of my anger and guilt for feeling jealousy over losing my baby status in the family that I was "bad." I also was convinced that I no longer belonged with my family or was wanted by them. I became the ignored or "lost" middle child, who tries to be perfect so that someone would notice and love me.

My father did notice, and he used me to make himself feel better. For as long as I made straight A's, I was someone he could be proud of and brag about. He never required such "graded" perfection of my other siblings. However, if I showed any signs of losing or lowering my mask of outside perfection, I would come under his anger. So the idea of there being two parts, or two sons, within me was *very pronounced*. As I grew older this separation between the two parts of myself became even stronger.

### God Does Not Argue

In college, I finally dropped any pretense of living up to my father's expectations, and he turned against me, humiliating me in front of an older relative, who had once molested me. At that time, I became thoroughly convinced I was totally "bad," and believing so, the Universe provided me with situations in which I could act out my "badness." I was so angry at not being loved unconditionally I felt that if my parents thought I was bad I would just prove how bad I could be. Yet I tried to, even then, keep many of the things I did from them – still unable to take their total rejection.

Finally, I decided I had to leave home and remove myself from this repressive environment or I was going to kill myself. I went to my mother and told her I wanted to transfer colleges and go to school in another state and complete my degree. My mother had become concerned about my emotional health and so she found the courage to go to my father and convince him this was something I needed to do.

### The Far Country

So, I became "liberated" so to speak, but as they say, when you leave one place the one thing that goes with you is *you*. Therefore, I did not escape the feelings of "badness." However, this distance from the watchful eyes of my fundamentalist parents allowed me to live a life where I felt I could breathe, but at the same time, I lived at the edge of the "hippie, free love" movement, which certainly could be equated with the Bible's "riotous living" in the story of the Prodigal Son.

### Prodigal Son

My contemporaries and I were angry over the Vietnam War and the old morality our parents had forced on many of us. We had all realized there was something seriously wrong in *Leave It to Beaver* land or *Father Knows Best* land. Still, my shadow side hung over me like a dark cloud I could not ignore. Not only was what I was doing "bad" or "wrong" in my parents' eyes, I was still feeling like the "outsider." And the Universe was there, supporting my being on the "outside."

There were times I literally did not have enough to eat from spending money on clothes. Though I was literally hungry for food, I was trying to fill up a hole left in my soul by my not being able to be who I was as a child. Even when I had started college, my mother still oversaw what I wore. So to take what little money I had and to be free to spend it on sexy clothes was a great joy to me. Even though I didn't think about what would happen when I didn't have money later.

### Why We Are in Want, and No One Gives to Us but Ourselves

My parents would send me $15 per week and I had a part-time job on campus, but I found that a good way to get to eat was to date or have a steady "boyfriend." So I can relate to the Prodigal Son's being envious of the bean pods the pigs had to eat in the story in the Bible because I was often in "want." In the translation of the Prodigal Son I read no one gave him anything to eat, and in my own life, I realized if I didn't do the romance thing, I wouldn't have anything to eat either. I felt God, at the least the idea of God that had instilled in me as a child, had deserted me a long time ago. So I saw myself in lack and saw only an "outside" source as fulfilling my needs. So I felt I was truly separated from any true sense of God and myself during this time.

### The Fallen Man

After falling in love with a man who really was a good man and who tried to help me in many ways, my parents came to the state in which I lived and accidentally found out I was staying with him. Well, I couldn't have fallen any lower in their eyes at that point. They hardly said a word to me on the 150-mile journey back to their home. After that school break, I am sure I could hardly wait to return to the "far country" to get away from their judgmental attitudes again.

### The Citizen of the Far Country

Later, my young man decided to marry someone else and deserted me, leaving me to feel abandoned once again. However, I soon found a husband to take his place. My husband made me feel safe in a world where I felt I had been abandoned and abused. He was big and strong and I felt he would never let anyone else hurt me. He became my true "citizen of that country," who helped me to start seeing some Truth. He literally picked me up and made a place for me. Of course my parents were overjoyed. Someone was going to marry their "soiled" daughter and they wouldn't have to worry any more about a scandal coming out because of my "bad" behavior.

### And Took His Journey Into a Far Country

My husband, bless him, soon realized I had tons of emotional problems but he was determined to make our marriage work. He decided to take a job out west four years after we married and right after we had our first baby. It was the first time I was living more than 180 miles from my family, and again, they deserted me. Terrified, alone, and with a brand new baby, I wrote and wrote home. Almost no one wrote back – ever. Finally, I was terrified that my husband would leave me too and I developed Agoraphobia becoming almost totally dependent on him.

### The Great Awakening

I started my great awakening by first attending a liberal Presbyterian church. There I started learning that God, *maybe*, was not like the one I grew up with. However, there was still too much of the judgmental thing operating within that church, of intolerance of homosexuals in elder positions, which set off my feelings of "unworthiness" and not belonging anywhere. I saw myself as like the homosexuals, okay to hang out with, but when it came to serving God the door was suddenly slammed. I was depressed when I went to church and after hearing the minister's sermons about how bad we all were as a Nation to have caused the terrible things that had happened in South America, happening at that time, it just made me feel like checking off the planet entirely.

Finally, I was referred to a Religious Science Church. Here I started to realize God wasn't that old frightening concept I grew up with and God wasn't like my father either. I went to this church for years, just sitting and soaking in what I could get on Sunday morning. I took a few classes, but nothing heavy duty in

Science of Mind. I was still filled with a lot of anger and feelings of abandonment.

**Self-Condemnation**

Though I kept being drawn to metaphysical religion, I was sure I wasn't good enough. I'd carried that message with me for so long that even when I thought I was over and done with it, it would crop up again.

Though my husband has been a great protector and provider, I still felt lonely. So I got involved in writers' groups and created the emotionally supportive "family" I never had through the members of those groups. Still, I was looking for someone outside of myself to make me feel happy. I thought I had found that person in several friends in my writers' groups, but they all went sour when they proved to be even more unstable than I was.

Finally, I thought I had found the perfect friend in a woman I'll call "Gloria." But she turned on me and told me I "was not worth" her time and that she *didn't* have the time to teach me what I needed to know spiritually. She also laid into me about my sister for my having been jealous of her and hating her for taking my place when she was just an innocent little baby. This woman friend really reamed me out. I was devastated. I lay in bed, curled in a fetal position, feeling terrible for days. I thought I would die with the pain.

**And the Father Saw Him Afar Off**

Finally, that Divine spark within me, which never dies, arose in me and told me that Gloria was wrong. That I did have worth. However, I felt that she was right about my sister and that I owed my sister an apology. I called my sister and told her about our older relative having molested me. She was horrified, but at the same time, wondered if that was why she had been miserable her whole life and she wondered if something like that had happened to her too. She was in the middle of separating and soon divorcing her husband of over twenty years. I made my apology, though she didn't understand it, saying I was her sister and she loved me. For a short time, we supported each other, but soon we went back to our old ways of having our own lives and little contact. Still, this seemed to be the opening for me to move forward toward a new realization about God and a new life for myself.

### God Does Not Condemn

It was soon after that a new minister came into my life. Something drew me to take classes with him, and I told myself if I was ever going to do this, take the classes, now was the time. Though I had completed a ton of work with counselors, I also knew somehow intuitively it was the time for me to get well completely – to heal on deep levels. I still had a lot of stuff to work through, but my new minister showed me over and over – that God does not condemn. With each class, I grew stronger, dropping old anger, sadness and moving forward. I soon learned almost everything I had been taught about God as a child was not true and I had been living my life based on beliefs which were false.

### God Knows No Sin

After starting practitioner training, I started seeing my life as the "hero's journey," which is basically the same story as the Prodigal Son. However, what I further found out was that not only did God not know or recognize sin, but that those parts of myself I had seen as "bad" or "shadow" material also were important to making me the unique expression of God that I am.

I came to the conclusion, or Truth, that God did want me, even me, to allow Him to speak through me and I shared this with my fellow practitioner students. I know that because of my experiences there is almost nothing a client could reveal about their life which would shock me, especially as to their feeling they have "sinned" or feeling that they were "unworthy." I feel sort of like Paul in the Bible, who had killed Jews, but God chose to speak for Him, showing how one can come back from the "dead" side of oneself. "For this my son was dead, and is alive again; he was lost, and is found."

### The Best Robe

When I presented my eulogy for practitioner class for my own memorial service, which was one of our assignments, I dressed myself in gold, an outward sign of my having chosen God and God's having chosen me.

### The Father's House Is Always Open

What I have learned is that God never deserted me. I realized I had never known God, but when I came to Know, then God was there for me. In fact, it has long been clear to me that God had been guiding me in spite of my journeys in and out of the "far country" or what I term as our "wasteland." If I had never been there, I certainly couldn't tell others of its value or write about it. So I give thanks for this experience and everything that ever happened to bring me to this point of growth and for propelling me forward into knowing the Truth about myself and the Truth about God – that we are not separated and never have been.

### The Stay-at-Home Son

Yes, I still get down on myself when I slip off the path and behave in a manner I don't feel is enlightened. But I am learning to spontaneously forgive myself. And to know when I get to that point of spontaneous forgiveness of myself I can learn to spontaneously forgive others.

It seems sometimes it isn't that dark side of myself which needs to be kept in line, but it is the judgmental side of myself which is really the part so unlike my God-self. I think it is very clear we often seek the sacred moment or the sacred part of ourselves in places or behaviors we think are "holy" and ignore *the sacred* that is staring us in the face – though it may be looking back at us with dirt on its face, having eaten the swine's bean pods.

## PRAYER TREATMENT WHICH GREW OUT OF THE PRODIGAL SON AS OUR STORY
*"Happy" Shaw*

**Purpose:**

To release any misgivings one might have ever had that God does not love and to know that God loves each individual so much that each one has been chosen, through self-choosing, to be an instrument of spiritual teaching.

**Recognition:**

There is nothing wondrous but God. God is beaming. God is beautiful and God is light. God pours out love, which is manifested in many forms. The forms are often so different we wonder at their usefulness. But God knows. God smiles and is happy.

**Unification:**

God smiles on me. God smiles through me. God likes me a whole bunch. God likes me so much that It decided to make me. Make me. Out of Itself. That's a whole lot of liking. It goes into Love. God loves me. God loves me.

**Realization:**

God loves me so much It has made me, me. I know this about God and God knows this about me. We are living through each other. When I speak, God speaks. When I breathe, God breathes. I cannot help but to speak of God, as I am God, speaking as me.

**Thanksgiving:**

I give thanks for me. For God in me. For God as me.

**Release:**

I have long since given up any idea that does not support who I AM. So it is and so I let it be.

**got spirit?**

*My Notes On The Prodigal Son As Our Story*

# SECTION TWENTY-ONE

# The Spiritual Path

*"One step at a time is sufficient for even the longest journey. It is not necessary to finish the journey in one day."*

– Johnathan Roof, Pathways to God

## My Crooked Path
*Rebecca Allen*

My path to this day has been crooked and twisted. Even looking at the journey from today's perspective, I have to be filled with awe and wonder. "Who would have thunk it?" My journey has been serious, but seldom solemn, Spirit has sent some unlikely, irreverent teachers.

There have been two underlying issues, which have intertwined and threaded their way throughout my life. One issue was that I was stupid. I laugh about being thrown out of kindergarten because I wanted my bears and dogs to be colored red and green rather than the standard brown and black. I knew the difference in the colors; I just thought brighter colors were prettier. That act of rebellion got me labeled as immature and uncooperative. Translated in a four-year-old's mind, "stupid."

In retrospect, I know I was hyperactive or ADD. Those were not popular issues at the time I was growing up. I was just told I wasn't trying hard enough when in fact, I know I was trying very hard but I just wasn't getting it. I must be "stupid."

I operated with that belief system until I was 30 years old. I was a sad, scared, hopeless, pathetic mouse of a person – inept, ineffective and shamed.

Then, Spirit sent me a savior, my Prince Charming, a balding, paunchy, middle-aged saint of a man, Jim Allen. Jim Allen had the insight, the wisdom and the authority to suggest that, no only was I not stupid, I was, in fact, *smart*. Bells rang, angels sang, the heavens opened and I was dizzy with the almost inconceivable possibility that I was smart.

Unconditional love and acceptance are powerful aphrodisiacs. The saintly Jim Allen and blooming Rebecca were wed and life happened – good times and bad times; ups and downs.

Ten years later, Spirit sent another unorthodox messenger in the form of a janitor. This young man worked for us and went to

## got spirit?

college. He was a nice young man, but he was not a rocket scientist. My young janitor, however, did not know that he wasn't rocket-science material. In fact, he told me he was majoring in physics.

Physics! Bells, angels singing, that dizzy feeling came over me. If this young janitor could go to college and major in physics, maybe I too could get into college. So, based on the courage I gained by comparing myself to this young man, I secretly took myself off to apply to the University of Southern Colorado. Surprise – I was accepted as a conditional student because my ACT test scores were low. That was okay; I was only going to take a couple of courses.

One major reason I wanted to go to school was to learn more about physics. I thought physics held clues to the universe and if I could understand something of the universe, then I could know more about God. If this young janitor could take physics, I too might be able to take physics and learn more of the universe.

More blooming. After a few classes I discovered I really liked college, in fact, I was doing very well and I decided to stick it out and get a degree. My physics teacher told me about an honors program she though I might want to take.

It was in the honors class that I met my guru. Let me say up-front, I despised my guru. This professor turned out to be a slight, impatient curmudgeon. He seemed intolerant of frightened, foolish people, in other words, he was intolerant of me. As head of the honors program, however, my guru professor was doing amazing work. He was teaching metaphysics.

Other seekers-of-truth tell warm, gentle stories of the wise guide who opened the door to their awareness. In my case, the door to my awareness was jimmied open. My guru professor and I were two individuals selected by the Universe to fight it out for a dubious prize – my soul.

Over a two-year period, my guru professor took my values, beliefs, and judgments, put them into a sack and shook them up.

## got spirit?

When I peered into the bag, everything was all stirred up and disorganized – especially me. Dr. Guru Professor had the audacity to suggest that I might be responsible for my own life. Frankly, that is a concept that scared me to death.

My professor guided his students through an odyssey of intellectual and spiritual exploration. Most of us were reluctant travelers. New ideas are scary and dangerous. We all often fight to hold onto old ideas, even if they don't work.

One fall day, in 1983, Dr. Guru took the class on a field trip to Denver to attend "Dimensions of the Mind," sponsored by a large metaphysical church. It was there that I received a free copy of *How to Change Your Life* by Ernest Homes.

It did change my life! I even came to love my cranky old Guru. I went to college to learn about the universe and maybe know more about God. Not only did I learn about God, I got a transformation! Isn't *Life* delicious?

The other causal theme, which has woven its way through my life, is about financial abundance. This is an issue that I am still jousting with, but it looks as though I am making progress.

As the old cliché goes, "I've been rich and I've been poor and frankly rich is better." Money has come to me in large abundant measure, yet I manage to think of myself as "lacking," therefore, I skip back into lack.

What I have come to realize is that there are two deep beliefs operating around my money issues.

The first is tied to my "you're stupid" belief. I have gotten the idea that stupid people don't deserve financial abundance. I frequently have "stupid" relapses. It takes some powerful self-talk to regain a hold on being smart enough. Stupid people aren't good "enough," therefore they shouldn't have "enough." A deep part of me believes also that one has to be smart to handle money.

Recently, I heard something on TV about the "good old days." It occurred to me, in a deep meaningful way, these are the "good old days" for me. If I didn't have my money issues, I would be in bliss.

I am connected with Spirit on a level, which I have never experienced before. In my hypnotherapy service I am doing work I love – work filled with meaning and purpose – work which helps people connect with their deep, powerful selves. At my work at a bookstore, I am free to read anything I wish and I get to meet interesting people who have interesting ideas.

Spirit has answered my prayers around my family. That saintly Jim Allen is exploring his spiritual beliefs, he is sober and content. My children are happy, well adjusted and productive. My mother is healthy. As a family, we are close, congenial and cooperative. I have a spiritual community to verify my beliefs and to facilitate my continued spiritual growth.

However, recently in the middle of the night, I sat up with a start. I had one of the major "Ahas" of my life. My aha had to do with all of this contentment. I realized I am functioning on a very old superstition.

As a child, I saw all of the adults around me dealing with hurt and sorrow. My grandmother lost two sons; my grandfather was disenfranchised from the family; my dad was chronically ill; my mom worked outside the home; a relative was drunk all the time; another was mean and was doing odd things to my cousin. I remember thinking that it was no fun to grow up because grownups only had work, worry and sadness.

Watching the adults, I learned to believe that no one can go through life without hurt, sorrow or pain. "Into every life some rain must fall."

Now, here I am as an adult. I'm really having too much fun. How dare I? I'd better manufacture some worry. On some level, I feel guilty about having so much good in my life. A stupid person does not deserve to have so much good, therefore, I'd better unload all the money before the gods of hurt can catch on and really give "you something to hurt about."

# got spirit?

Financial lack is a very safe sorrow to have. It is familiar to me. I know how to do broke-and frankly-I do it very well. *If I stay in a poverty mode, then maybe some of the other horrible tragedies will not befall me.*

This was a recent revelation. I am still sorting it out. Of course, I can tell myself this is a foolish belief, but it is very deep. It feels like the next layer of an onion.

I must convince myself of two things. First, I must know on a deep basic level that I create my reality and if I want to create a perfect life, I may. There is no outside god of sorrow who is looking for fresh victims. If sorrow comes to call, it is an invited visitor – I can choose to thumb my nose and refuse to answer the door.

Second, I must know that I am good "enough." I must know that not only am I smart; I am wise. I must know that I can trust myself to create a perfect life. I must know that I am God in action and the portion of God that I represent deserves all the good in the universe.

As a student of the Spiritual, I am gaining in grace each day. It feels like there is a deep settling of belief. Truly and sincerely, I can see that although my path has been convoluted and twisted, I am thrilled to be in this place, at this time – these are the good old days. My life is overflowing with good. And, so it is and so I let it be.

## My Spiritual Journey: Coming to Know a Power Greater Than Myself

*Tammy L. Young*

I have come to know there is a Power greater than I am that is guiding and protecting me in all my affairs. I have not always known that. I have also come to realize that this Power has been with me from the beginning. I once looked upon my past as a terrible burden I had to bear. I have blamed others for a great deal of pain and confusion in my life. Now I no longer harbor any blame or resentment for the past. I see everything differently now, through glasses of a new color.

I know in past times that were painful, Spirit was watching over me and protecting me. I see now that no permanent damage was done. I see now that all my life's events have lead me to this beautiful and perfect place in my life. I now am able to see the Divine Source of all life; I can look in retrospect and know Spirit flowed through me and around me and through all of my affairs. I see the perfection in what I once saw as horror.

As a young adult, I believed God had abandoned me. I always believed there was a God, but I was very angry with God. I believed in life that was painful and desperate and loveless. My first "adult" choices were made in desperation and in a search for love in a loveless life. I worked myself into a frenzy with two forty-hour-per-week jobs at the age of sixteen. I worked for money and I worked to relieve the sense of worthlessness I felt and I worked to prove to others I was not who they thought I was.

At seventeen, I married a young man who truly loved me. This marriage was another act of desperation to fill a void in my life – what I felt as a lack of love. It was my belief then that life was loveless and when I saw someone could love me, I latched onto that without hesitation. It only took a short while to realize this young man's love could not fill my void and I could not fill his. Perhaps a divorce at the age of 19 was a step in the right direction. It was movement, nonetheless. I had a strong inner urge to find what I was looking for *out there*.

At this point in my life, I decided I didn't *need* anyone, except Nickolas, my two-year-old child. Surely, I thought, he alone could fill the void and I could figure out this thing called "life" and everything would be okay. Again my sense of lovelessness and desperation took over and I immediately became involved with an older man. This relationship was both abusive and addictive. This person was addicted to me, he was addicted to speed and he was addicted to violence. He reinforced my belief in a loveless life and my victim mentality. With him I confirmed no one could truly love me and I was to live a life without love.

I held on to Nickolas as my emotional support. It never occurred to me what I seemed to lack was within me. I blamed. I blamed the man, I blamed my parents, and I blamed myself. But that inner knowing, that urge to grow and to change was always present. As I dipped my toes into the gutters of life, I knew there was something better. It was only a matter of knowing that I deserved it and that I could find it. What I now know to be INNER GUIDANCE is what pulled me out of this horrible relationship. At the time, I called it "inner strength." I spent ten months in this situation and had a second child. One day, I packed a diaper bag and left. I had left many times before. This time I never returned. Hooray for me! This was a genuine turning point in my life. I once defined it as hitting rock boom. I don't define it in those terms anymore. I realized that even if life was loveless, I was not so unworthy that I needed to risk my life every day and the lives of my children. I was barely twenty years old.

I came to Albuquerque to stay with the only person left to help me. I had a very limited support network in those days. Many people had tried to help and to great expense and heartache, I had let them all down.

However, this one friend was still willing to believe in me and help me find a new way. Once in Albuquerque, I talked my way into a good job and made another act of desperation, a plea for help. I called a therapist out of the phone book who talked with me for an hour. I told her I could not afford her fee. She gave me a reduced fee and we made an appointment for the following Saturday. I worked with this therapist every Saturday for a very long time. In many ways, she saved my life. She helped me to return to sanity and to see that though life had dealt me some bad hands, I had done well in many ways.

Most importantly, she helped me to see the pattern of choices I was making as an adult. I found then that I was in a desperate search for love. It was during this time that I met a new man, and my therapist helped me navigate through a new courtship. My therapist always questioned my intentions and helped me not to act in desperation. I finally felt like a functional person. Eventually, our sessions became every two weeks until finally I discontinued them, anxious to navigate on my own.

I had changed my beliefs by degree, but had not yet made a complete shift in consciousness. I still believed love was in short supply for me. I saw myself as limited. My therapist had helped me to find a certain degree of peace in the abandonment issues I had with relatives and she had helped me to reconcile the guilt and the blame. We had not addressed my feelings of abandonment by God. Obviously, we never talked about God. I still believed that God had left me hanging. I was angry that God created a horrible mess in my life and then turned a cold shoulder to the needs of my soul. I felt this tremendous void, but I was unaware that it could ever be filled.

The new man in my life took me to a new thought church and what the minister there said about God and who I am appealed to me. I wanted to believe it; it sounded good. So, I hung around. I began to develop a belief in myself that had never existed before. I began to believe that I was strong! I was a survivor! I was going places! This was certainly movement in the right direction. Later, with much practice, these beliefs became so embedded in my mind that I left no room for anything else. I allowed no vulnerability in my life.

In my new couple relationship, there was no sensitivity. I would not allow myself to be hurt by him regardless of the outcome. I determined that I would not rely or depend upon him. I would never allow myself to need him because I was strong. I could do it all on my own. At the time, this approach to our relationship was good for both of us; we had an unspoken agreement that fit both our needs.

After three years of a relationship marked by struggles for independence and the fight against dependence of any kind, I made perhaps my last act of desperation. I married him. I thought I loved him, but I was not capable at that time of love at a Soul level. Mostly, he loved Heather, my daughter. Heather was a difficult child from birth. My new husband and she had bonded from the very beginning. He is and always was her father. They knew it and I knew it. He wanted to raise her and to be her father. He wanted to raise both of my kids. I simply came with the package. I'm not sure how aware he was of this, but it was very clear in my mind.

I feel now that I married him out of desperation because I was afraid I would never be presented with this attractive of a deal again. He was incredibly handsome. He loved my children. He was a responsible adult. He was sophisticated and educated. He wanted very little from me really.

I knew that with this man I could build a good life. It was a good decision by all appearances. I elected to overlook the fact that he did not love *me*, that we had been on a roller coaster ride for three years with periods where we really didn't even *like* each other, and that there was no real intimacy between us. I married him for my children because I did not believe I could ever again find a man so attractive who would be willing to marry me.

And I was comforted by the fact that I was so *STRONG*. I had lived the last twelve years in absolute turmoil and this was better

# got spirit?

than that – *so it must be right.* After all that I had been through, surely I could handle this. This decision is a perfect demonstration of my belief in a loveless life. There could be love for everyone else in the world. There was love for my children and for my new husband and for everyone else. But there was no love to be found for Tammy. I was willing to live with this because it was my belief. It was my truth. It was my identity.

I had another baby and our life together was not too bad. I developed a more extensive support network. I always had my strength! I had become very busy. From the time I was sixteen, I have always stayed very busy. I know that my *busy-ness* was, for a long time, a way to avoid dealing with life on an emotional or spiritual level. And we faced some hardships in 1993. We had not built the kind of relationship, which would enable us to really face them together. We had done well the year before when we almost lost our baby. We had tried to be a team and comfort one another. I felt supported at times and still abandoned at others. I think the experience helped us to develop some intimacy, but it was not enough for what lay ahead. It seemed in 1993 we were holding it all together. Then, in 1994 we experienced a real tragedy.

On June 30, 1994 we were in an automobile accident. I was the only one injured. I sustained a closed head injury – a traumatic brain injury. The effects were minimal in medical terms. In life terms, the effects were massive. Everything I ever thought I was existed at a head level. I was my strength. I was my determination. I was my independence. I was my intelligence. On June 30, I was no longer any of these things. I was badly hurt and I had no one to help me.

My husband was angry that I had changed so much, and he didn't understand or believe my injury was substantial. Again, I felt abandoned. Only this time, it was the most intense abandonment I had ever faced. The injury took away everything I thought I was.

I became depressed and suicidal. It was not until late August that I found help at a rehabilitation hospital. I was treated for my injury and began to climb out of this horrible tunnel. I worked with a psychologist who helped me to remain sane, but assured me that my marriage would end once I recovered.

The biggest turning point in my life came one day on a hospital bed during a cranial treatment. I was suddenly floating at the top of the room. I sort of existed above it. I wondered briefly if I was dying but knew I could not leave my children. I experienced a love and a bliss I had never known existed. I was at peace for the first time in my life. I was cradled by a loving, peaceful entity. I knew in that moment everything was going to be okay. I knew I would be okay. This experience lasted for about 30 minutes, but it was an eternal moment. I became aware that all that I thought I was before the injury was not me at all. I realized I did exist as a Spiritual being. This was a powerful realization for me. It caused me to begin a spiritual path.

As my husband and I struggled to redefine our relationship, I enrolled in a class, which was supposed to help me put my life in perspective and help me plan my future course. I looked for reasons for this injury, a lesson to be learned. It was not easy to find. I had not been on this journey long when my minister announced he would be leaving the church to retire. I was crushed. I was again flooded with feelings of abandonment. Later, when I heard the new minister, I knew I had not been abandoned. I knew somehow that our new minister could help me get to where I wanted to go. I enrolled in more spiritual classes and just continued through them and was finally licensed as a practitioner four years later.

It has been an incredible journey of love and enlightenment. It has been painful. My personal transformation had a tremendous impact on my marriage. In many ways the marriage improved and there were times we experienced the greatest joy of our twelve years together. However, I was eventually confronted, by the ways in which I had compromised myself in our relationship and eventually I came to realize I was no longer the person who had created the relationship I was in. I was living a life in which I could no longer function.

Perhaps the most difficult decision I've ever made was the one to leave my marriage. It was painful and scary, but I knew in my heart that it had to be done. My journey continues. I have established the truth of my being. I know who I am now and I know that I am a spiritual being expressing love and light. I know that there is, indeed, a Power greater than I am that has always been with me and always will be. I know that I have not ever been abandoned. I know that there is an abundance of love in my life.

The challenge before me now is to allow that love to unfold in my experience without repeating my pattern with a fear-based belief that I will not attract exactly what I want and need in a relationship. Then I can simply allow that love to show up without attempting to force it into being.

I have three wonderful children, am now a successful author of my own book, a very capable teacher of special needs children and a spiritual practitioner. Now, I know that Spirit has been with me all through my journey and my love for myself and others has blossomed. I am truly blessed and grateful to now know that there is so much love and so much beauty to be experienced. And my heart is open to it all.

My journey is not complete, though I have awakened to the truth of my being. The rest of my life is devoted to a greater understanding of this truth for myself and for all those who seek my help.

### PRAYER TREATMENT
*Tammy L. Young*

***Purpose:***

To know that I am guided daily by the Ultimate Intelligence of the Universe. In every situation, conversation, decision, and intention, to know I am Divinely Guided. To recognize Divine Guidance as It is always present within me. To give up questioning the origin of my intuition. To give up questioning the outcomes. To follow my intuition with faith in a Power greater than I am to guide me in all things – great and small.

### Recognition:

I am surrounded in this moment by a Divine Presence. The Presence is within me; it is all around me. It is the One. This One is Intelligence. This One is Wisdom. This One is Love. This One is Perfect. This One is all there is!

### Unification:

This One is within me and I am within It. I am One with it. It is my Source and my Sustenance. I am One with all that It is. I am Love. I am Wisdom. I am Intelligence. This is my Truth and my Reality. It is *WHO I AM*.

### Realization:

This Wisdom and Intelligence is within me right now and always. In every moment, every situation, every decision and every intention, I am guided by the Divine Presence within me. I know instinctively how to manage my affairs. I follow my intuition and allow it to lead me to my highest good. Divine Love within me speaks the truth of my being through me in all of my affairs. In every conversation, in every situation, I allow Spirit to speak for me, through me, as me. I live with assurance that every idea, every intention, every decision is of a Divine Nature and is from the One. I follow my intuition with faith and trust in the Perfect Source of my being as my Guide.

### Thanksgiving:

I give thanks for the intuition that is inherent within me. I am grateful for the free flow of Divine Intelligence through me. I give thanks for these truths and this teaching.

### Release:

As I have spoken these words, they have entered into the Law of my Being and have already been manifest. And so I release them now with the very need for this prayer. And so it is.

# SECTION TWENTY-TWO

## *Closing Prayer*

## Closing Prayer
*Barbara Fox*

*I open my heart to the overflowing current of love.*

*I allow it to bathe my spirit, my cells, and my mind.*

*I am fully aware of my Oneness with Spirit.*

*I lovingly release that which is no longer the truth of my being.*

*I lovingly bid farewell to all thoughts, ideas, resentments, grudges, prejudices, fears and concerns and fill my heart with the spirit of Divine Forgivingness.*

*I forgive other people, places, and institutions.*

*I forgive myself.*

*I allow the love of Spirit to fill me with an ever-increasing awareness of Truth.*

*I know that this Truth is eternal and unchanging. As I walk in this Truth, my path is clear and I touch those around me.*

*And so it is.*

## Authors Bios

**David Alexander** grew up in metaphysical religion and at an early age began working with youth. He is now a licensed Religious Science Practitioner, a youth advocate, and a ministerial student in the Mid-West.

**Jeannie Bullard** has been a marketing executive and nutritional consultant, as well as a massage therapist. Currently, she is a real estate agent and a licensed interfaith spiritual counselor residing in Scottsdale, AZ.

**Rebecca Allen** is a licensed hypnosis therapist as well as a licensed Religious Science Practitioner. She is the host of a television program on alternative healing methods which is aired in Albuquerque, NM.

**Lynne M. Curtis** lives with her daughter in New Mexico. Teacher, nurse and motivational speaker/presenter, she is committed to living life just beyond her comfort zone. She has served as a nurse in Brazil and the US. Possessing a great sense of humor, she is often a guest speaker at churches and seminars.

**Barbara Fox** owns her own recording studio and has been a radio personality, dj, and an audio book tape reader. She is also a licensed Religious Science Practitioner and has been a 12 Step sponsor for many years.

**Dave Shultz** was reared on a dairy farm. He received his BA/MA in Civil Engineering at the University of Wisconsin. During his 32 years with the USFS, he worked in WA, OR, AZ and NM. Currently, he is a private consultant in developing community based partnerships, a licensed Religious Science Practitioner, father of four grown children, and grandfather of two. He is passionate about helping people and communities discover their own unique gifts, strengths and choices. He resides in Albuquerque, NM.

## got spirit?

**Tammy L. Young** is a licensed Religious Science Practitioner, teacher, author and educational consultant. A teacher of special needs children, she has published a book on honoring the spirit of the ADDHD child. She and her three children reside in Austin, TX.

**Kay Lewis Shaw a.k.a. "Happy" Shaw** is an award-winning teacher, artist and writer, whose writing has appeared in national magazines. A former literary agent, she is known as a master teacher of writing. She is a life-time honorary member of Southwest Writers. Currently, she is a licensed interfaith counselor, publisher, and ministerial student who is frequently listed in Who's Who of American Women.

**got spirit?**

Correspondence to any of the authors should be mailed to:
Remington Literary Associates, Inc.
10131 Coors RD NW, Ste. I 2-886
Albuquerque, NM 87114

Please enclose author correspondence within a separate inner envelope for fowarding. Please include author's name on inner envelope only.

## Copyright Acknowledgments

The editor and the authors express acknowledgment to the authors and publishers of the following copyrighted material, which may have been briefly quoted or mentioned within some of the essays or highlighted section quotes. We highly recommend to the reader all books listed here as illumined works helpful to all on the spiritual path.

1. Beattie, Melody. **Beyond Co-dependency.**
2. Butterworth, Eric. **Spiritual Economics.**
3. Chopra, Deepak. **Creating Health, The Seven Spiritual Laws of Success.**
4. Chodron, Pema. **Awakening Compassion, Good Medicine, Pure Meditation, When Things Fall Apart.**
5. DeAngelis, Barbara. **Real Moments.**
6. Dyer, Wayne. **Your Sacred Self, You'll See It When You Believe It.**
7. Emerson, Ralph Waldo. **Essays.**
8. Goldsmith, Joel. **Practicing the Presence, The Thunder of Silence.**
9. Hay, Louise. **You Can Heal Your Life.**
10. Hopkins, Emma Curtis. **Scientific Christian Mental Practice.**
11. Holmes, Ernest. **Science of Mind (Textbook), How to Use the Science of Mind, Living the Science of Mind, Creative Mind and Success, This Thing Called Life, This Thing Called You, Beyond Appearances, Effective Prayer**
12. Jeffery, H. B. **The Principles of Healing.**
13. Kuebler-Ross, Elizabeth. **Death and Dying.**
14. Levine, Stephen. **Who Dies.**
15. Moore, Thomas. **Care of the Soul.**

16. *Palmer, Parker J.* ***"Leading from Within,"*** Noetic Science Review, Winter, 1996.
17. *Rapoport, Judith.* **The Boy Who Couldn't Stop Washing: The Experience & Treatment of Obsessive-Compulsive Disorder.**
18. *Roof, Jonathan.* **Pathways to God.**
19. *Sinetar, Marsha.* **Elegant Choices, Healing Choices.**
20. *Troward, Thomas.* **The Edinburgh Lectures on Mental Science, The Creative Process in the Individual.**

## Other Recommended Books Or Audio Tapes

1. *Braden, Gregg.* **The Isaiah Effect, The Lost Mode of Prayer.**
2. *Chopra, Deepak.* **The New Physics of Healing.**
3. *Kornfield, Jack.* **Meditation for Beginners.**
4. *Caroline Myss.* **Why People Don't Heal.**
5. *Hanh, Thich Nhat.* **The Present Moment.**
6. *Watts, Alan.* **The Book: On the Taboo Against Knowing Who You Are.**
7. **A Course In Miracles.**
8. **The Holy Bible.**
9. **The Holy Quran.**
10. **The Kabbalah.**

Printed in the United States
3672